GW01398971

FROM BEDFORDSHIRE

Edited by Dave Thomas

First published in Great Britain in 2000 by
YOUNG WRITERS
Remus House,
Coltsfoot Drive,
Woodston,
Peterborough, PE2 9JX
Telephone (01733) 890066

All Rights Reserved

Copyright Contributors 2000

HB ISBN 0 75431 937 7
SB ISBN 0 75431 938 5

FOREWORD

This year, the Young Writers' Future Voices competition proudly presents a showcase of the best poetic talent from over 42,000 up-and-coming writers nationwide.

Successful in continuing our aim of promoting writing and creativity in children, our regional anthologies give a vivid insight into the thoughts, emotions and experiences of today's younger generation, displaying their inventive writing in its originality.

The thought, effort, imagination and hard work put into each poem impressed us all and again the task of editing proved challenging due to the quality of entries received, but was nevertheless enjoyable. We hope you are as pleased as we are with the final selection and that you continue to enjoy *Future Voices From Bedfordshire* for many years to come.

CONTENTS

Naomi St John   1
Zahed Ahmed   2

Ashcroft High School
John Ndikum   3

Harrold Priory Middle School
Rachael McLuskie   3
Jenna McKeown   4
Emma Chatfield & Jennifer Eardley   5

Lea Manor High School
Lenna Craig   5
Lynsey Head   6
Carl Philpot   6
Kirsty Scrivener   7
Daniella Mullings   8
Louise Hughes   8
Rachel Hart   9
Liam O'Sullivan   10
Stephen Ring   11
Stacey Howarth   11
Aaron Boutwood   12
William Goode   12
Andrew Tate   13
David Mitchelmore   13
Kayleigh Redmond   14
Oliver Quantrill   14
Laura Warren   15
Aimee Louise Iveson   16
Kitty Chan   16
Chanda Patel   17
Krissy Reeve   17

Linslade Middle School
Melanie Derbyshire   18

Luton Sixth Form College
                    Arpana Pattni   20

Manshead Upper School
                    Claire Narracott   21
                    Leanne Spark   22
                    Dawn Taylor   22
                    Sarah Oatham   23
                    Daniel Mayoll   24
                    Stephanie L Cain   25
                    Scott O'Sullivan   26
                    Samantha L Dunbar   26
                    Victoria Blair   27
                    James E Taylerson   28
                    Daniel Short   29
                    Samuel Dear   30
                    Maxine Anderson   30
                    Andrew W Kitt   31
                    Katherine Brown   32

Mill Vale Middle School
                    Chloë Sydes   32
                    Kenechi Oji   33
                    Matthew Hurren   33
                    Natasha Wilson   33
                    Kavita Siyodia   34
                    Matthew Tuffnell   34
                    Stephen Nunes   34
                    Daniel Vass   35
                    Karen Taylor   35
                    Bruce Lennox   36
                    Stacey Miah   36
                    Paul Russell   37
                    Amy-Claire Short   37
                    Joanna Doublett   38
                    Donna Jones   38
                    Leana King   39
                    Andrew Custance   39

Stuart Jones   39
James Morris   40
Jamie Irons   40
Sophie Hooper   41
Rebecca Lewry   41
Chris Taylor   42
Nadia Ahmed   42
Victoria Smith   42
Ross Edwards   43
Kyle Mackenzie   43
Laura O'Reilly   43
Pierina Penny   44
Andrew Robert Bland   45
Rachel Chambers   46

Northfields Upper School
Carly Church   46
Hayley Taylor   47
Amy Kennedy   48
Jamie Murray   49
Sharon Tonks   50
Scott Jenkinson   50
Nichola White   51
Leigh Ireson   52
Daniel Norman   52
Wade Stanton   53
Lisa Homans   53
Tim Parker   54
Rachel Allwood   55
Caroline Impey   56
Ryan Bartlett   56
Hayley Vardy   57
Ryan McNamara   58
Donna Lumsden   59
Fiona Broni   60
Becky Roberts   61
Brenden Delaney   62
Lisa Taylor   63

Emma Clapham	64
John Owens	65
Carl Budd	65
Amy Burke	66
Stacy Hutton	67
Michael Greenwood	67
Sarah Steffens	68
Louise Rowles-Griffiths	68
Lawrence Willis	69
Matthew Bandar	70
Ricky Parker	71
Katie Neal	72
Nicola Botcher	73
Larissa Sheehan	74
Declan Hanley	74
Charlotte Haines	75
Paul Murphy	75
Greg Winter	75
Matthew Moleski	76
Chris Boyle	76
Danny Bright	77

Queensbury School

Adam Croft	77
Leander Moore	78
Geoffrey Baines	79
Lisa Ayres	80
Paul Crane	81
Natasha Moulds	82
Fabienne Morris	83
Russell Fairfield	84
Kelly Yeung	85
Kirstie Morgan	86
Emily Farley	86
Jenny Pooley	87
Roshni Siyodia	88
Laura Wells	88
Caroline Tilley	89

Ruth Gray	90
Caroline Peak	91
Samantha Taylor	92
Alice Tunmore	93
Nicola Golding	94

Redborne Upper School

Sam Antoine	94
Amy Walker	95
Andy Purkiss	95
William Nixon	96
Gemma Brandom	96
Natalie McCaffrey	97
Alix Courtney	98

Rushmoor School

Alex Hill	99

Stratton Upper School & Community College

Kai Griffiths-Shilton	99
Jennifer Stead	100
James Scott Davies	100
Alexis Cormano	101
Keiran Williams	101
Jacqui Hart	102
Clare Pulling	103
Nicola Massey	103
Samantha Hope	104
Naomi Peters	104
Daisy Whitbread	105
Gareth James	106
Donna Jakes	106
Mary Orchiston	107
Lyndsey Garrill	108
Alicia Harrison	108
Danielle Braybrooks	109
Rachael Head	110
Rachel Louise Morris	111

Leanne Hough   112
Collette Marie Norman   112
David Vaughan   113
Phillip Bartlett   113
Holly Dennis   114
Natalie Jayne Pearson   114
Ben Lawrence   115
Lisa Bly   115
Tom Sizer   116
Vicki Coles   116
Jenny Willett   117
Ben Bastin   118
Steven Harrison   118

The Cottesloe School
Julia Shields   119
Russell Pritchard   120
Sophie Burgess   120
Louise Davies   121

The Poems

NORTH WIND

frosty morning cold
creeps rapidly to my door
a gash in the wood
offers admittance
her winter breath is frigid
it sharply slays my breath
a gust of wind blows out
the embers fierce gold
perishing coals
slowly dull to ashen grey

i force myself to rise
the cold hits me in a frenzy
i hurry to the door
a grey sock
i thrust into the gap
the north wind is gone
at last

later sitting before
the glare of the open fire
clasping a mug of tea
i smile at the encounter
with north wind

Naomi St John (13)

WHY?

Pearls of wisdom fall from your lips,
Rivers of love flow from your heart,
You are the phoenix whom death cannot defy,
You appease my misery,
With divinity in your smile.
Heavenly abstinence through such provocation,
How you bear my selfish thoughts.
You see a friend,
But you I do not know,
Lives apart yet our souls are still searching.
I glide through my dreams,
Only to find hope awaiting me,
Trapped in this tunnel,
Your light guides,
But I close my eyes,
I cannot see, will not see; do not want to see,
So why love me?

Zahed Ahmed

WAY TO SUCCESS

When the moon high above,
and the stars far away,
Gracefully light the way to my home,
I look up at the wonders,
High in the sky,
And the joy that they bring to my heart.
But when I reach for a goal,
There is no moon to look up to,
No light to lead my direction.
Where there is no path
That is where I must walk,
And a trail I shall leave right behind me.

John Ndikum (13)
Ashcroft High School

IMAGINE

Imagine there's no happiness
It's easy if you try
No beautiful surroundings
And no clouds in the sky
Imagine there's no colour
And nothing else in sight.

You may say I'm wicked
But I'm not the only one
I think you'll see just what I mean
As the world has just begun.

Rachael McLuskie (12)
Harrold Priory Middle School

School Rules!

I trudge along the pavement
I'm on my way to school
Some say that it's not so bad,
I disagree with them all.

You see - they don't cope with bullies
Like I've always had to.
They come to me with questions
Like 'Do you know what to do?'

I mean - how would I know?
I don't know this stuff!
I just copy from books and read
Picking from my toes, fluff!

They don't have to go home at five
After staying late at school.
I'm just too tired to go to the pub
And play a game of pool!

They don't have to mark school work
Or tell other kids to go faster
They don't have the problems I have
After all - they're not the *headmaster!*

Jenna McKeown (11)
Harrold Priory Middle School

IMAGINE

Imagine there are no planets, floating in the sky
No flowers to grow
No kites to fly
Imagine all the people who were living yesterday,

Imagine there's no air to breathe, no clouds high above
No sunshine to light the day
No birds, no eagle, no dove
Imagine all the people in poverty and war.

Imagine the world in sadness, no smile, laugh or grin
An everlasting war
Wishing a happy life to begin
Imagine there's no tomorrow to talk about today.

You may say that I am morbid
No feelings for anyone
I live alone in my own dark world
No day, no light, no sun.

Emma Chatfield & Jennifer Eardley (11)
Harrold Priory Middle School

MY NEW TEACHER

My new teacher is kind, helpful and friendly,
My new teacher has a low voice that is like a bird singing
                                                      when we are good.
My new teacher has short blonde hair like the sun,
My new teacher dresses nicely like a flower.
My new teacher is thin and tall like a stem,
My new teacher is nice. Can you guess who it is?

Lenna Craig (11)
Lea Manor High School

MY NEW TEACHER

My new teacher has a mountain of things about her,

Some are funny, some are sad
Some are good and some are bad.

She sings like a bird
also shouts like a gorilla.

Her teeth gleam like crystals
in the sun.

Although she may have four eyes,
there's nothing wrong with that!

She has a few freckles here and there
but that's a part of here.

She can also speak French
'Je m'appelle' she may say.

But at the end of the day she is funny,
Can you guess who she is?

Lynsey Head (11)
Lea Manor High School

MY NEW TEACHER

My new teacher is as scary as a wolf.
His teeth are as sharp as a Tyrannosaurus Rex.
His voice booms like a gun shooting or a volcano exploding.
Sometimes he is happy but only when we do things right.
He can stomp as loud as an elephant.
He can jump as high as a kangaroo.
Any idea who?

Carl Philpot (11)
Lea Manor High School

MY NEW TEACHER

My new teacher is a woman
Well-educated and wise.
She has shoulder length hair
And big blue eyes.
Blondish brown is the
Colour of her hair.
She is a good teacher,
my new teacher is fair.

She teaches two lessons
and has four posters on the wall.
She is of a medium
build and is fairly tall.

She has teeth that are
cared for and that
sparkle in the sun.
She is really hard on homework
So I make sure it is done.
She has a sense of humour
and just like my mum
she makes learning easy cos
she makes it fun.

My teacher dresses smartly
But she is not all that.
I wonder if you've guessed it yet,
My new teacher is Mrs . . . Batt.

Kirsty Scrivener (11)
Lea Manor High School

WHY?

Guns going off, bombs exploding buildings,
Everybody's dying, everybody's trying.

Nobody wants to be friends,
They just want the world to end.

I'm tired of these wars,
What is the cause?

In Indonesia they're having a bad time,
I'm sitting here writing a rhyme.

Why is all this happening?

All these strangers,
Putting families in danger.

All these people being accused,
I'm becoming very confused.

Why can't people live a normal life,
Without destruction, guns and knives?

Why is all this happening?

Daniella Mullings (12)
Lea Manor High School

THOUGHTS

Traipsing through the slush on a cold winter's day,
Just thinking of my little Anne back home hiding in a corner,
Hearing the crashing of the bombs.

Just hearing all the bangs worried me that I might never see her again,
That I might never be able to hug my little Anne.

The killings go on, one after another falling to the ground,
Like a cemetery of disposed bodies.

Seeing all these bodies made me think that it might be me next,
Just a slight glance away could leave me in the darkness.

Louise Hughes (12)
Lea Manor High School

THE FOOTBALL MATCH

I woke up in my bunk, freezing cold
A blanket of snow lay across the ground
Untouched by any soul.
I got my breakfast - a stale biscuit
Someone had nibbled that.

Then I spied a Gerry
Grabbed my gun and ran to get Hopkins
We stood by the trench exit
but he shouted out to us
'Merry Christmas'
We were so surprised
He came up and gave us a neatly wrapped parcel.

Later on that day
A football match was arranged.
Us against the Jerries
A very jolly game it was
Then we exchanged gifts.

The next day we started fighting again.
They killed my best mate.
This time it was Hopkins.

Rachel Hart (12)
Lea Manor High School

THE BULLY

As I was walking to school one day,
I heard a nasty harsh voice say,
'Oi you, yes you. Get over here,
Or feel the pain of a slap round the ear.'

I walked on pretending I didn't hear,
Deep down inside, I was trembling with fear.
Thoughts of humiliation ran through my brain
The stark realisation of oncoming pain.

I could hear his voice shouting ' Just you wait
Tomorrow you'd better not be late.
I'll kick you, then chuck you in the river,
Then pull out your heart, your kidneys and your liver.'

His absurd speech made me burst with laughter
Then I stopped for I knew I would pay for it after.
The humour came to a halt when I thought what he
Might actually have in store for me.

Dozens of butterflies were in my belly,
My legs felt as if they were made of jelly.
I was trying hard to get it out of my mind,
This bully wasn't about to be kind!

The next day I went, but he wasn't there,
And it wasn't as if I didn't care!
He was gone. I was brave. I thought 'He's a fool.'
I jumped at the chance to get straight to school.

I found out the reason. It was very bad.
He'd been rushed to hospital: a row with his dad.
Now I've come to appreciate
Bullies are victims who express their hate.

Liam O'Sullivan (13)
Lea Manor High School

MEN AT WAR

It's the night before they go out and fight,
They're worried.
They lie in the trenches,
It's smelly,
There are rats,
They have no food at all.
Suddenly there is a huge explosion,
And they hear gunfire.
They have a look.
There are soldiers dying
And there are people crying,
They lie still worried,
Because soon they'll have to fight,
They don't want to die
And they don't want their families to cry.
But soon they will have to fight
And they don't know why.

Stephen Ring (12)
Lea Manor High School

WHY?

It was Christmas Day and for once
All was quiet
And the English came from the trenches
So the Germans came out from the ground.
They put their guns on the floor.
Doesn't this show that war did not
Have to happen?
Men didn't have to die
Women and children didn't have to suffer
But still the war carried on.

Stacey Howarth (12)
Lea Manor High School

WHY WAR?

Up the ladder of death and over the trench.
And for what, nothing at all
Gunfire, explosions, a blank mind
As I climb the ladder.

Then happy memories of home but
Then back to reality.
I'm running
Running away from death but
He gets closer and closer.

I cheated death for today but
Will he get me tomorrow?

Aaron Boutwood (12)
Lea Manor High School

PEACE

On one very special day in the war
love and care came between them,
As therefore it was *Christmas Day*.

On that day they had a football match.
No war,
Just a clean, nice, unarmed game of football.

No one cared if you lost or won -
England or *Germany*.
After a nice game
They went back to the trenches.

William Goode (12)
Lea Manor High School

THE GREAT WAR

Tomorrow we trudge up to the trenches,
To fight for an unknown cause,
We were told to fight against a deadly enemy,
For the sake of all England.
So we go and fight and kill a man,
Who was doing what he was told to do,
A man with friends, a wife or maybe a family.

We could have killed his friend earlier,
One quick shot with my gun.
His commanding officer, his acquaintance,
I could have killed not knowing I had ruined his life,
But he could have killed my friend or my chum.
I'm taking revenge on a man I don't know, as if it's his fault,
He could be thinking the same of me,
I could have killed his son.

Andrew Tate (12)
Lea Manor High School

THE GREAT WAR

It's Christmas Day,
I'm happy in a sad kind of way,
The killing never stops,
The endless slaughter goes on and on.

My friends fall like chickens shot in the head,
The food's great here, we have the same every day.
Rock and slush are our four-course meal.

Cold and dark with no blanket, just smells of the dead,
But all over that I still smell home
And then I am reminded why I'm here.

David Mitchelmore (12)
Lea Manor High School

THE TRENCH

It is dark and cold, the soldiers are tired,
The rain falls down and darkens the town,
Guns going bang as the fighters ran.

Daylight was coming round the corner,
The English and Germans come out of the trenches,
'Fancy a game of football?' They say,
'I mean, it is Christmas Day.'
They play the game all friendly and nice.

The day passed by and another one dawned,
The fighting continued yet again,
Red blood running down the drain,
People screaming again and again.

'No more' they cried, but the war went on,
Family and friends now have gone,
Bodies scattered among the hills,
But still the shooting took place.

Kayleigh Redmond (12)
Lea Manor High School

MY NEW TEACHER

My new teacher has a voice like roaring thunder,
His eyes are beady as a marble
And glow like a wolf's.

My new teacher has teeth as white as a lion's,
He's very energetic,
With speed as fast as a panther.

He's a very helpful teacher.
Can you guess who he is?

Oliver Quantrill (11)
Lea Manor High School

FOREVER

Trudging to the trenches was all they could think about,
For tomorrow it would happen,
And that's where they would go.
With rotten boots,
Trembling with the cold.

Dizzy with thoughts they did not want to think,
Firing,
Fighting,
Killing.

Ready,
Steady,
Go!
Running from the trenches,
Yelling, screaming, dying.

I got one - *Bang*,
They got one,
Run, back!
Back into the trenches - *Bang! Bang!*

Gas!
Quick, run,
Somebody stumbling got caught in the gas,
Nobody could forget - they all wanted to.

Next day again we will trudge to the trenches,
And the fighting will start once again,

We will probably die in the morning and so it will go on,
over and over again.

Laura Warren (12)
Lea Manor High School

THE TEACHER

My new teacher has a very loud voice,
like an exploding volcano.
He has sharp teeth like a lion.
He teaches information technology
and is always smartly dressed,
like a business man.
He walks around the room
like a cheetah running to catch his prey.
He likes to help you,
like he is a gorilla nursing its babies.
He likes to keep our fingers typing,
like we are secretaries working for him.

Can anyone guess who he is?

Aimee Louise Iveson (12)
Lea Manor High School

IN THE BATTLEFIELD AND TRENCHES

In the middle of the battlefield
I sat in the trenches and watched
Soldiers shooting back and forth, back and forth.
Hurt in the trenches, I lay cut and bruised.
Tired from restless sleep, hungry and starving.
Deaf to sounds, apart from bombs.
I look up and get ready to shoot.
One, two, three, I pulled the trigger
And shot a person in-between the eyes.
Feeling guilty, I went back into the trenches.
I looked beside me and there was a bomb . . .

Kitty Chan (12)
Lea Manor High School

WAR

We're fighting in the trenches,
Muddy, stodgy sludge,
My boots are now rotten,
I'm fighting in the war.
My arm is bleeding like hell.
My best friend's been eaten by rats,
But still the war goes on,
I haven't got a clue why.
One more day until Christmas,
Please let the war end.
I want to go home to my family
And open our presents together.
It's Christmas Day today,
We've shook hands with the Germans
And played a game of football.
The day is nearly over - will the war start again?

Chanda Patel (13)
Lea Manor High School

FEAR

The noise is ferocious
Of gunshots and fear,
Fear.
The fear of death.
I was lying on my bed,
Watching the rats chew on my best friend.
Tears were running down the sides of my face
Of sadness and regret.
It's my turn tomorrow,
It's my turn to die,
Goodbye.

Krissy Reeve (12)
Lea Manor High School

I HAVE A DREAM

I have a dream . . .

That in the future homelessness and hunger will be forgotten,
War and fighting will happen no more
And disease will be wiped out.

All dreams and hopes will be conquered,
People will help others whatever their needs
And all the time words would be used like 'thank you' and 'please'.

All countries will come together and prevent global warming,
Murders and crimes of all sorts will disappear.

There would be no more forest fire
And animals won't lose their habitat.
Senseless killing of animals would be yesterday's news
And winners won't laugh in front of those that lose.

I hope that in the future Girl Guides and Scouts will be full up
And people won't be obsessed with money and greed,
So the rich can help those people in need.

Schools would put a stop to bullying,
So fights would be abandoned, like kicking and hair pulling.

All newspapers would only print good news
And most of that would be achievement.
Money won't be one of the issues
And every year everyone would give up something for Lent.

In my dream litter and pollution is not a problem
And graffiti will fade.

Brothers and sisters would not fight
And divorces won't be made.

Streams would be supplied with fresh, clean water
And drought will stop.

Tornadoes, hurricanes and earthquakes will not happen
And neither will famine.

In my dream robots will have taken over housework and cleaning
And none of them will go berserk!

Everyone would have a perfect pet and wild animals will run free.

That is my dream.

Melanie Derbyshire (12)
Linslade Middle School

THAT SPECIAL BOND

You've grown up with them,
You've been through thick and thin,
But where you'll end up,
The future looks dim.

You'll remember the laughter,
You'll remember the joy,
You'll remember the arguments,
Over that good-looking boy!

As you grow,
You'll find you drift apart,
But always will remain,
That special bond within your heart.

For you know you'll never forget,
The memories you once shared,
Knowing it will soon all end,
You're hurt, you're upset and you're scared.

It will never be the same,
You're sure to separate,
You'll meet new people here and there,
It's destined as your fate.

But your paths will cross again,
It's in your destiny,
That special bond will once return,
That bond between you and me.

Arpana Pattni (16)
Luton Sixth Form College

MY DISABILITY

A large disabled symbol carries me around,
An unwanted companion,
But a necessary presence,
In my disabled world.

My lonely, bare universe,
Contains only me,
Solitary is my being,
Except for my machine.

No one dares to enter,
My nightmare life,
People try to ignore me,
Seeing my deformed shell.

Why do people ignore me
Please tell me why?
If only my body worked,
So I wouldn't be denied.

Loneliness fills my life,
My body, my soul,
No one wants to know,
A twisted, deformed beast.

Claire Narracott (13)
Manshead Upper School

FOREVER, FOREVER

Feel my heart beat,
With your soft hands,
Always pumping,
Forever, forever.

Will you be there?
Just like my heart,
Next to my skin,
Forever, forever.

Waking each morning,
Wherever I am,
Just to be here,
Forever, forever.

Thanking the Lord,
Being with you,
Will it be,
Forever, forever?

Leanne Spark (16)
Manshead Upper School

CAMERA SHY

I'm just a foal who's newly born
And nervous as can be
For someone's got a funny box,
They're pointing it at me.
They're up to something,
I'll be bound
That box, it makes a 'clinky' sound!

But my mum she doesn't seem to mind
In fact, she's staying cool and calm.
She knows about that clinky box
And wouldn't let me come to harm.
So if I snuggle close and tight
I'm sure that things will be alright.

Dawn Taylor (14)
Manshead Upper School

FOOTSTEPS IN MY DREAM

Sometimes I listen to see if I can hear the footsteps
of the man I have only dreamed of.
I think that he will appear to save me if I listen hard enough,
but I'm so crazy about him that I can't picture a thing,
I finally found my man standing in the shadows overlooked by my
trustworthy friends. How can I light an end to this torture?

A million times that I feel nothing I can deny, but when you hold me
close I feel I could fly. In the corner of my heart I see a space with your
name on it, darling, if only you could realise the love we could have
would be so strong, I would never string you along.
Sometimes I wish I could be somewhere else, someone else so you
could see. Give me a chance to make this right, the time has come
for us to unite, dreams I can wish for but reality prevails.

Oh why is it the prosperous people find love? I'm trying so hard
but all the smiles I have won are now dead and the tears have come
back that I shed all those years ago.
There's nobody in this world that could love you more than I would,
I'd be here for you. For bad or for good, I will be here.

Sarah Oatham (14)
Manshead Upper School

My Heart, My Life, My Story

I wonder lonely down a street thinking about life
It struck me that it had been very hard
Many people don't stop to think about sufferers
But I know what it's like, as I've seen it all before.

I started as a little cutie, as all mothers say
But there was already a problem in my life after a few days
My parents were very worried and it was going to be rough
And as for me it has been very tough

Since I first knew about my problem I have been seen a lot
Trundling down the corridors, wondering what was next
I was scared many a time over the next few years
In and out of hospital, check-ups always near

Then about nine years from the start, I heard some good news
I was about to be mended and cleared of my faults
One last ultrasound and another ECG.
My hole would be filled, my life would be complete

After the operation I was under a lot of stress
My chest was left open and far from my best
I kept thinking about going home even after receiving
All the gifts that were given, it all seemed deceiving

As now I am better, healthy and well
There have been good and many bad spells
It's becoming hard work now as I'm getting older
And now I will not have to worry that my life will become shorter

Now though, there is another trouble in my life
The thought of divorce gives me a fright
In a kind of way I am not too bothered where it all ends
As long as my life delivers what it sends.

Daniel Mayoll (14)
Manshead Upper School

CRYING IN THE RAIN
(In memory of James Heley, 1985-1999)

If I could go back,
I'd do it gladly.
Back to last year,
Before all the waiting,
Before all the hurt.
Back to that night
In the bowling alley,
A life so changed since then.
Between now and then,
Is a void.
Eight months of worry,
Eight months of wait.
Everyone warned me,
Everyone knew.
Not me though.
I had faith,
But where did that get me?
He was a person,
Who touched my life.
I can't let go,
I can't forget.

Stephanie L Cain (14)
Manshead Upper School

MONEY

Money.
Why does the world revolve around you?
An inanimate object,
Small,
Unattractive,
With a portrait of the Queen
As if she owned you
The two Ps line my piggy bank like pebbles on the beach.
So many sparkling in the sun,
And still,
After writing this,
I will go out
And scramble in the never-ending cycle
To make more of this
Power-possessing problem,
That I call
Money.
Why does the world revolve around you?

Scott O'Sullivan (14)
Manshead Upper School

SMILE

We all smile
        Our motives differ
I smile
        Does anyone notice?

A beaming smile
        Can be false
It shines like the sun
        What is the reason?

Oh, to be smiling all of the time
        Your face would stick
Happiness is certain
        Does it last?

My smile, wide and giggling
        I do it every day
Special, a grin from ear to ear
        Why do I smile?

Samantha L Dunbar (16)
Manshead Upper School

MY LOVE

Looking at you now in a whole new light,
If only others knew what we did that night.
Being with you there was magical, but real,
We tried to stop ourselves but can't help how we feel.
Since you entered my life my world has been brighter,
I'm your cigarette and you're my lighter.
When two hearts beat as one like ours,
We don't need money or flashy cars,
We just need each other to cherish and love,
I'll be your hand if you'll be my glove.
I'll be your coat for those stormy winter days
And I will be here for you always.
Your are my moon, my stars, my sun
And to me you are the only one.
No matter how far we are apart,
You will forever be in my heart.

Victoria Blair (14)
Manshead Upper School

I VALUE LIFE

I value life and all it has to offer,
Lots of others say, 'Why do people bother
To live life to the max and try their hardest
To be better than the rest and look their smartest?'
But I wonder why these people think,
That life has no point but we should all drink,
To the pleasures of life and how it brings pleasure.
Even though all things in it are not made to measure.
There are lots of sayings that make you laugh,
Like 'Life is like a hot bubble bath,
The longer you stay in the more wrinkled you get'.
That's true though so do not forget.
When you have children, make them laugh, make them sing
And make them enjoy life, as it is a one-off thing.
Remember to tell them what it was like in your day,
As we cannot forget the old tradition, but anyway,
Getting back to the point that I made at the beginning,
You must treat life like it is a new thing.
You must value life and all it has to offer,
Ignore other people and make sure you bother,
To live life to the max and try your hardest,
To be better than the rest and look your smartest.

James E Taylerson (13)
Manshead Upper School

THE TANK

Bullets whizzing past my head,
Most of my friends are already dead.
Enemy shots keep getting near,
But I still don't have a fear.

Moving along on my caterpillar feet,
Looks like my side's gonna get beat.
The men inside me load me to fire,
They move my cannon to aim higher.

Bang! There goes my deadly shell,
Our leader shouts 'Give 'em hell!'
The explosion, like a thousand lions
Their manes rising up into the heavens.

But from the back there comes a loud bang
And then like fog, the silence hangs.
Enemy tanks at six o'clock!
The ground beneath me starts to rock.

Then we turned to fire back,
But my hull suddenly went crack.
Into the deadly flames I sank
And that was the end of me, the tank.

Daniel Short (14)
Manshead Upper School

WHEN GOD BECAME MAN

No room at the inn,
Born in a wooden stable,
Only Son of God.

Innocent baby,
Lay asleep in a manger,
Saviour of the world.

Shepherds saw angels
And left flocks on the hillside,
Saw the Lamb of God.

A star overhead,
Showed the wise men the birth place,
The light of the world.

Gold, frankincense, myrrh,
Gifts fit for a baby King,
A present from God.

Hope for the future,
He showed us the perfect life,
When God became man.

Samuel Dear (14)
Manshead Upper School

A WINTER'S POEM

As I was walking in the woods
With the wind whistling through the trees
An owl was hooting in the moonlight
The sound echoing in the breeze.

As I was walking in the woods
The leaves crunched beneath my feet
Small animals scurried on the ground
And the branches made a creaking sound.

As I was walking in the woods
I shivered with cold and fright
It was eerie with all these sounds
That the woods would make at night.

I ended walking in the woods
When I reached my door
It was so quiet in my cottage
A silence I'd not heard before.

Maxine Anderson (14)
Manshead Upper School

WAR

The purpose of war, I know not,
All I know is that it is to kill,
Two countries can't get along, what a thrill,
This is the purpose of war? I think not.

The thing is, war sorts out these problems,
But the way it is done,
Both countries should be hung,
But is this the only way to sort out all
these problems?

No talks are possible,
Just brutal killing,
Why can't they just shake hands and sign
the writing?
Why aren't talks possible?

Look what is left behind all because of war,
Dead bodies and bulletless guns,
Mind you don't tread on the innocent ones,
Look what is left behind, all because of war.

Andrew W Kitt (13)
Manshead Upper School

PREJUDICE

Black and white on the bus,
Each sits down without a fuss.

Young and old, strong and weak,
Prejudice, blame we're always to seek.

Rich and poor, we're all the same,
Everyone here is to blame.

Disabled or able, thick or thin,
Everyone has committed at least one sin.

Muslims, Jews, Christians too,
Everyone's the same in God's own view.

Katherine Brown (14)
Manshead Upper School

MY POEM

How does the Earth stay round?
By drawing a circle with compasses.
Why is the Earth round?
It was the way God wanted it.
Will the Earth stay round?
The Earth will end up half a circle because
The animals ate half the Earth.
Where will it be in 100 years?
Disappeared into the atmosphere and never to return.
Who will discover the next incredible thing?
I will.
Is the world so great?
Mine is.

Chloë Sydes (12)
Mill Vale Middle School

A FUTURE POEM

Is that a time when war will cease
and around the world will bring about peace?
Is that a time cars will be moving off the ground -
no crashing, no accidents but safe and sound?
Is that a time when humans can fly
to different planets or to the sky?
Is that a time death will be no more?
Will these things ever happen?
Somehow - I do not know.

Kenechi Oji (12)
Mill Vale Middle School

I SHOULD LIKE TO . . .

I should like to take away a part of Mars
I should like to hear the wind whisper
I should like to paint the thought of an animal
I should like to understand the meaning of life
I should like to see my grandchildren in years to come.

Matthew Hurren (11)
Mill Vale Middle School

FUTURE THOUGHTS

I would like to see an alien from another planet.
I would like to hear animals speaking English.
I would like to understand how our great world works.
I would like to take away horrid creatures - wasps and snakes.
I would like to paint the giggles that a joke can bring.

Natasha Wilson (12)
Mill Vale Middle School

A Futuristic Poem

How will we travel in the future?
Spaceships will take us far and wide to all places different.
Where will we be living?
In bubble houses on the moon, Earth will be as bare as a rock.
What will food be like?
It will be made from our imagination.
What will aliens do when they visit Earth?
They will be our friends and stay here forever more.

Kavita Siyodia (12)
Mill Vale Middle School

I Would Like To . . .

I would like to hear the roar of a dinosaur,
I would like to see the rebirth of a dodo,
I would like to understand the unexplained,
I would like to take home a ray of sunlight,
I would like to paint a picture of a lion getting along with a deer,
On a hot summer's evening in a field full of long grass in Africa.

Matthew Tuffnell (12)
Mill Vale Middle School

I Should Like To . . .

I should like to paint a moving creature in the dark night.
See the breeze on a hot summer's day.
Hear the rustling of leaves on a windy day.
Understand the rage of an angry buffalo.
Take away the ripples of water on a lake.

Stephen Nunes (11)
Mill Vale Middle School

THE MYSTERIOUS FUTURE

How do the leaves fall?
With a quiet, drifting sigh.

How does space keep the planets in?
With a hug of darkness and an ongoing power.

Where do the tooth fairies live?
Behind the cavity in molar 4!

Where did Shearer get his goal celebration from?
From the sheer confidence and energy in his toes.

Will the sky ever fall down?
If the air supply stops and the world stops spinning.

What will happen in the future . . . ?

Daniel Vass (13)
Mill Vale Middle School

FUTURE VOICES

Will dinosaurs ever walk the Earth?
Only in our dreams.
When will people grow wings?
When apples dance and oranges sing.
Will robots ever rule our planet?
Only when hairbrushes speak.
Will there ever be giants taller than trees?
Only if they eat lots of cheese.
Will there ever be life on Mars?
Why don't you ask the aliens!

Karen Taylor (12)
Mill Vale Middle School

FUTURISTIC POEM

In the year 3050 will we be using cars?
Either cars of flying beauty, flying close to Mars.
Where will fairies sleep at night?
In a cotton sock with a fair ray of light.

Will birds still soar through the sky
Or will they watch and see other things fly?

Will we go to work or will we stay at home?
The world is our oyster and for us to roam.

Will we be ruled by aliens with big, black, googly eyes
Or will we be able to rule our own personal lives?
Will we eat food and drink
Or will we have tablets as small as a blink?

Bruce Lennox (13)
Mill Vale Middle School

A FUTURISTIC POEM

Will there ever be a day when we don't go to school?
In someone's imagination may be.

When will cars fly?
When they are ready to come off the ground.

Where will fairies live in the year 3000?
In a house at the bottom of the garden.

Will humans ever fly?
In their dreams perhaps.

When will we be able to do all these things?
Somehow I don't think we will ever know.

Stacey Miah (13)
Mill Vale Middle School

FUTURE VOICES

I would like to understand
the powers of Hell.

I would like to see
a unicorn fly through the sun.

I would like to paint
my wildest dream.

I would like to hear
the Grim Reaper calling the
ghosts from their graves.

I would like to take away
the eyes from a hairy beast.

Paul Russell (11)
Mill Vale Middle School

MY FUTURE WISHES

I would like to see people who are poor
build houses and eat healthily.
I would like to hear the whistle
of the wind and trees.
I'd like to paint the misty
winter's morning dew.
To understand what
goes on in our lives.
To take away the killing and murder
in the world, to animals and humans
every day.

Amy-Claire Short (11)
Mill Vale Middle School

FUTURE WISHES

I should like to see a fox awaking.
To see it blink in the sunlight.
I would like to hear the clouds move,
And hear the sun burning.
I would like to paint happiness
on Christmas morning,
Happiness as a gift, is unwrapped.
I would like to understand
people's feelings,
Why we laugh and why we cry?
I would like to take away the
sound of children singing,
The sound of voices in the streets.

Joanna Doublett (12)
Mill Vale Middle School

FUTURE VOICES

I should like to take away
a rain cloud from the sky,
I would like to paint the
vision of love and happiness
of the children,
I would like to see the
whistling of the wind.
To hear a web which has
just started spinning,
To understand the
never-ending of space.

Donna Jones (12)
Mill Vale Middle School

I SHOULD LIKE TO . . .

I should like to take home
the rays of light on a frosty morning.
Understand the rage of the wild sea,
the fury of a stormy night.
I should like to paint
the relief of a problem solved.
I should like to understand
all the mysteries in life.

Leana King (11)
Mill Vale Middle School

I SHOULD LIKE TO . . .

I should like to paint the noise of a woodpecker pecking.
I should like to see the feeling of happiness.
I should like to hear the voices of the stars.
I should like to understand the meaning of life.
I should like to take away the singing of a bird,
Saving it until I feel lonely.

Andrew Custance (11)
Mill Vale Middle School

I WOULD LIKE TO . . .

I would like to paint happiness,
I would like to see the birds sing when the sun is rising,
I would like to hear the greatest view,
I would like to smell the finest chocolate,
I would like to take home the most fantastic memory.

Stuart Jones (11)
Mill Vale Middle School

I WOULD LIKE TO . . .

I would like to see the moon shine down
On a quiet, dark and dusky evening.
I would like to hear the sound of laughter
On a pitch-black New Year's Eve.

I would like to paint the sound
Of a bird waking up in the morning.
I would like to understand the vibrant shatter
Of a tree shaking in the wind.

I would like to hear the gentle cry
Of a litter of newborn cats.
I would like to feel the icy sea
Brush against my cold, bare feet.

I would like to see a shooting star,
Fly swiftly across the sky.
I would like to hear the hooting of an owl,
As I gently fall asleep.

James Morris (11)
Mill Vale Middle School

I WOULD LIKE TO . . .

I would like to see the wind that whirls around the world.
I should like to hear animals speak in English, just like us.
I would like to paint the sound of an electric guitar.
I should like to understand arguments and sort them out.
I would like to take away problems going on around the world.

Jamie Irons (11)
Mill Vale Middle School

I WOULD LIKE TO . . .

I would like to take away the clouds from the sky,
Making it look like a big blue pie.

I would like to understand the meaning of life,
Why a knife is called a knife.

I would like to hear everyone in the world laugh together,
As well as a voice of a swan's feather.

I would like to see the colours of the world unite,
As well as a happy and caring fight.

I would like to paint an unsolved question,
Just to see all the colours everyone would mention.

Sophie Hooper (12)
Mill Vale Middle School

I WOULD LIKE TO . . .

I would like to see the universe,
The stars glittering in the darkness.
I would like to hear the cheers from a crowd,
The voices dancing in my ears.
I would like to understand an animal,
The thoughts of a rabbit.
I would like to take away the trees and bushes,
The leaves rustling in the wind.
I would like to paint dolphins and whales,
The splashing of their fins in the water.

Rebecca Lewry (11)
Mill Vale Middle School

I WOULD LIKE TO . . .

I would like to see inside my body through a computer screen.
I would like to hear the sound of a solar powered car
                               pulling up into my drive.
I would like to take the wings off a bird and fly away to the moon.
I would like to paint the sound of the waves crashing against the rocks.
I would like to understand what it is like to be dead.

Chris Taylor (11)
Mill Vale Middle School

I SHOULD LIKE TO . . .

I should like to hear the constellations shimmer,
I should like to see the scent of exotic perfume,
I should like to take away the diamond-shaped stars in the sky,
I should like to understand the chatting of dolphins,
I should like to paint a ripple in the foreign seas.

Nadia Ahmed (11)
Mill Vale Middle School

I SHOULD LIKE TO . . .

I should like to hear the dew settling on green grass,
I should like to see the air with the scents that flowers make.
I should like to understand the laughs of a hyena,
I should like to take away the smell of freshly made cake.
I should like to paint the sound of a violin playing to music.

Victoria Smith (11)
Mill Vale Middle School

I'D LIKE TO . . .

I'd like to take away the pain of war,
I'd like to paint the sounds of running water,
I'd like to hear the sounds of the rainforest growing,
I'd like to understand the power of nature,
I'd like to see the World Wide Web reach out across the world.

Ross Edwards (11)
Mill Vale Middle School

FUTURE VOICES POEM

I should like to hear a dinosaur growing up
I should like to take away the smell of water
I should like to see the sound of laughing
I should like to paint an old tree falling
I should like to understand the twist of a tornado.

Kyle Mackenzie (11)
Mill Vale Middle School

I SHOULD LIKE TO . . .

I should like to paint the universe.
I should like to see paradise.
I should like to hear animals speak.
I should like to understand life.
I should like to take away the pollution of the world.

Laura O'Reilly (11)
Mill Vale Middle School

I Should Like To. . .

I should like to see Christ rise again,
Hear the angels singing.
I should like to blow bubbles and catch them,
Change history.

I should like to hear the clouds floating,
To touch the sun.
I should like to paint the sky,
Follow a rainbow.

I should like to paint the greenness of the earth,
The trail of an ant.
I should like to find the edge of the world,
To see a flower grow.

I should like to understand the purpose of living and dying.
Take away the fumes from a car,
Intimidation and fear.

I should like to reach the stars,
Catch the snowflakes,
I should like to paint a wave of the sea,
Change the world to a better place,
                    To treasure my dignity.

Pierina Penny (12)
Mill Vale Middle School

I Would Like To . . .

I would like to see a computer thinking,
All day long,
Never stopping and never looking up at me
Through the shining screen.

I would like to hear a Christmas tree
Talking
All day long,
Chattering and chattering all night
Has gone.

I would like to understand
An owl howling
All night long,
Carrying on all night long until the
Crack of dawn.

I would like to paint a bluetit red
In a silver tree,
Having three little babies.

I would like to take away
The fights
In the school playground
Having a nice peaceful break
To have a nice day.

Andrew Robert Bland (11)
Mill Vale Middle School

I Would Like To . . .

I would like to see the stars at day,
So that I can see them when I go and play.
I would like to paint the happiness of the sun,
To see what beautiful work I have done.
I would like to hear the flutter of a humming bird in a far away land,
Find how many gains there are in a cup of bright yellow sand.
I would like to understand the importance of life,
Ask why does a husband have a wife?
I would like to take the splinters out of wood,
Like the arrow in the tree shot by Robin Hood.

Rachel Chambers (11)
Mill Vale Middle School

Cats' Eyes

His eyes are deep pools of mercury,
His eyes are as black as coal,
His stare is deep and meaningful,
His stare is the bottom of the ocean.
His gaze is fixed with no movement,
His gaze is full of sophistication.
His eyes dance in the moonlight,
His eyes dance like fire.
His eyes, cats' eyes are burning,
Burning with sharpness so intense.
His eyes are staring at you,
Staring with a glare as you watch him,
Watch you.

Carly Church (14)
Northfields Upper School

INDECISION

A ghost of my indecision stares at me blank,
Watching, waiting, smelling the air so dark and so dank.
It's always there, making me scream,
Wanting to wake up from this recurring dream.

I close my eyes to block out the pain,
I open them slow, it's back again.
What it wants, I can't sacrifice,
But one day it will be thrown in these fateful dice.

And as I wait for my judgement day,
The lies and deceit don't crawl away.
They sit there festering, growing with mould,
Sitting for years, so grudging and old.

Yet, it's all so simple, it makes it hard,
I can't do it, I won't appease my heart.
And when I hear the sound of your voice,
Calling to me, I go without choice.

You're like an addiction, I can't control,
And without you I ache from deep within my soul.
And in you glide like a sunset night,
And I give it all up without a fight.

The ghost has won, I made my decision,
And in my soul lies a deep incision.
Everything goes away so slow,
I gave it all up, I let you go.

Hayley Taylor (14)
Northfields Upper School

THE TOUCH OF MOONLIGHT

The scream of a neighbour I used to know
A sickening thud as she fell to her death
A racking sob as a young man lay bleeding
An anguished moan as he took his last breath

I turned at the sound of her crying
A huddled figure encased in her fright
I smile and waved at my salvation
My precious daughter who lights up the night

It was then that I heard of the creaking
But by that time it was too late
The house came down as though to slaughter
And the silence whispered of my fate

My heart stood still - I was frozen
But my legs moved without word from my mind
And my eyes, and my soul began a desperate search
For what I was loathe to find

I knelt at the rubble I came to
And I heard a muffled cry
As a child's hand emerged from the debris
And reached up towards the night sky

As I knelt my wounds were unfeeling
As were the tears that I cried
And though I held her hand in the moonlight
It was in the darkness of my heart that she died.

Amy Kennedy (14)
Northfields Upper School

THE AIR WAS DEATHLY STILL . . .

The air was deathly still
Not a sound at all
The tears are streaming
The earthquake had hit

Through a small crack in the roof
I see the sun's rays beaming onto my face
Like a deep piercing beam
As I slowly release myself from the debris
Of my once humble abode
I realise that life itself will never be the same.

As I crawl through the ruins of my own home
And try to look for salvation
I realise that civilisation itself
Has been swallowed up in this, a cataclysmic disaster.

An eerie hush had descended upon the town
Which was only disturbed by an odd scream
Or shriek of fright and terror
For now it seems that the world is in peace and quiet.

A sudden creak and all becomes dark
A sudden crash and my world is over
And then suddenly silence
A sudden jolt and it's back again
Like a creature
With a relentless thirst for blood and death
And then all at once life itself is over!

Jamie Murray (14)
Northfields Upper School

MY STARS

I look into the skies above,
To see my stars, the ones I love,
Twinkling, sparkling, some big, some small,
How I would love to touch them all.
As the night proceeds, my stars shine bright,
I wonder if they'll shine all night,
Jupiter, Venus, they're all up there,
Living a life, full of no care.
Through my window I look beyond,
There is something between us, a special kind of bond.
As I stare up above the midnight sky,
I wonder how, and I wonder why,
My friends, the stars, they look at me,
And how they shimmer and how they gleam.
The morning sun now appears,
And now my stars begin to clear,
Until another night they come,
My stars and I will remain as one.

Sharon Tonks (14)
Northfields Upper School

GUNS AND BOMBS

All I can hear are machine guns,
We're just fodder for the bullets,
Bang! Bang! Bang!
Another three men dead.

Whee! Whee! Whee!
Bang! Booff! Whosh!
I see an enormous amount dead,
Form the whistling bombs.

Guns, bombs, gas,
All they do is kill,
Death, destruction, desertion,
War a pointless waste.

Scott Jenkinson (13)
Northfields Upper School

HUNGER FOR LOVE

The eyes of a child, born to die
to witness the horror and pain
living through hell each day of his life
then being forced to live it again

One lone tear, roll down a mud-stained cheek
The skinny arms reach out for your heart
and what can you do but walk away
but each time you tear him apart

Until the next time the young hopeful
sees light in someone's eyes
and gives his being, his very soul to them
to be shattered with all their lies

To walk this life alone, so young
I watch with tears it's so easy to see
that he my love so alone I hold out my hand
and say 'Child come with me'

And together we walked the plane of paradise
in the sweet cool heaven above
'And this is how it will be' I said to him
never more will you hunger for love.

Nichola White (15)
Northfields Upper School

HELL

I've always wondered what it's like in Hell
It could be like living in a huge cell
In which you could only come out at night
Imagine seeing the Devil, what a sight!

Who would you meet, Jack the Ripper?
Would you dare speak to him?
What about Adolph Hitler?
What would you say to that figure?

I wonder if there really is a Hell
If so, how many people live there?
Do they give newcomers a scare
Or give them a terrible dare?

I wonder what it's like in . . .
. . . *Hell!*

Leigh Ireson (14)
Northfields Upper School

TORNADOES

T earing up houses and trees
O ver the big blue seas
R ageing winds and a heavy breeze
N ow creeping forward like a mouse
A family afraid to leave their house
D roning sounds all through the night
O ne more life is claimed by fright
E ating homes and trees aflight
S ilence as it leaves our sight.

Daniel Norman (14)
Northfields Upper School

THE BLAZE

The flames eat away at the walls
Like ravenous dogs,
Engulfing the landscape like
An out of control twister.
Roaring like a lion,
The heat - unbearable.
It leaves its mark, the terror has gone.

Tiny sparks start the process once more.
The uproaring flames devour
Everything in their path.
Terror at the trail of destruction,
Like a disease spread across
A land filled with poverty.
Disastrous effects that the heat unveils.

Wade Stanton (14)
Northfields Upper School

LONELINESS

I feel upset when someone has died
I always run away and hide.
I feel lonely and scared sometimes,
Like I've been stabbed in the back several times.

Loneliness is a type of feeling
I lie alone looking up at the ceiling.
It can make me cry
And feel like I want to die.

To stop feeling lonely I call a friend
And after a chat I'm feeling on the mend.

Lisa Homans (13)
Northfields Upper School

THE FUNERAL

Sad faces fill the room,
A sombre silence fills our hearts.
Crying eyes survey the room,
This is the worst day of my life.

I'm so depressed,
I can't even cry.
I don't understand it,
Why did he have to go?

People say they understand,
How could they, he wasn't their dad?
All the sympathy for me, but why?
I'm not the one that's dead.

The vicar begins to speak,
It hurts to listen.
The man he's describing's a saint,
That's not my dad, he was fun.

He'd swear and curse when upset,
He'd break down and cry when sad.
But for all those failings,
He was still my dad.

Back at home, it's wrong,
It's sad and quiet.
It doesn't feel the same,
Now that my dad is dead.

Tim Parker (14)
Northfields Upper School

THE MARKET BEGGAR

Another day at the market,
Underneath the blistering sun.
On the warm cobbled floor,
He established his seat.

He lay down his rug,
And put out his tin
And took his place at the market,
For another day of begging.

The people strolled by,
As he clasped the stubs of his fingers,
And crossed the skeletons of his legs.

The crust of his hat once fresh and unused,
The mask of his jacket, moth-eaten and torn.
The skins of his trousers from the charity shop they came,
The shells of his shoes with vents in the soles.

People walked by without a care in the world,
Their fancy riches from afar,
Their life lived by the pound.

Children scurry past,
Led by their mothers.
Staring at his weakness, staring at his incapacity.

The market beggar rolls up his rug,
And peeks into his tin.
He has just scrimped enough for his bread and pie,
Until tomorrow . . . he is the market beggar.

Rachel Allwood (13)
Northfields Upper School

THE TREE

The tree just stands there,
Alone in the park,
People stand and stare,
It's been there for years,
Growing and growing,
Up to the clouds.

The tree doesn't like all the attention,
It wishes people would just walk by,
They stand and stare at the curving branches,
The rough old bark,
The bright green leaves.

There's nothing special about this tree,
It's just the only one you see,
All the others have been taken down,
To make way for this great big town,
Little kids ask their parents,
'What's that?'
And their parents reply, 'That's a tree,
The only one left in this town.'

Caroline Impey (13)
Northfields Upper School

SPACE

Space the final frontier,
Earth's people have wondered about it for years.
We know little about our universe,
Maybe it's because we are under a curse.

The solar system is made of planets and stars,
I would love to fly to Mars.
Mars is a red splodge in the sky
It looks like something out of a pie.

I would love to go to space,
I wish I was the first in the human race.
I would travel all over the place.
This is why I love space.

Ryan Bartlett (13)
Northfields Upper School

THE BORING LIFE OF A TIN PENCIL CASE

Normally, you'd think that a
    Tin pencil case can't think.
Well, normal pencil cases can't,
    But this one can breathe and think.

I've also seen one that breathes, thinks
    And talks, this pencil case loves holding
His breath, but one thing that it definitely
    Can't do is walk!

For two years, this pencil case has been
    packed fully to the rim and can last no longer.
The pencil case has had enough and now
    All that fills it to the rim is anger.

The pencil case has held his breath for too long
    And explodes. The stationery goes everywhere.
The student who owns the pencil case
    Doesn't even care.

Now because the pencil case didn't hold his anger.
    The impatient little tin pencil case
Can hold his breath no longer.

Hayley Vardy (13)
Northfields Upper School

HE IS THE SEWER RAT

He scurries along the sewers,
Focusing on finding food,
The smell in the air is disgusting,
But he still aims on finding food.

He puts up with hunger,
Until he finds food,
His life depends on finding food.
He is the sewer rat hungry for food.

Another day and still weary,
Another day and still scared,
Another day and still ready to fight,
Another day and still hungry.

He puts up with hunger,
Until he finds food,
His life depends on finding food,
He is the sewer rat hungry for food.

He has to scrape to get his food,
He has to have instinct,
And senses to find his food,
He has to be the hunter to find his food.

He puts up with hunger,
Until he finds food.
His life depends on finding food,
He is the sewer rat hungry for food.

He finds food and guards it with his life.
He drags it back to his lair
He nibbles it to keep him going through the night
He is the sewer rat a scavenger, a hunter and not hungry.

Ryan McNamara (13)
Northfields Upper School

ISOLATION

I'm drowning in a sea
of black memories.
This barrier I've built up
closes in on me.
I hear distant laughter,
but a wall stands between
them and me.

Constantly calling but no one hears,
endlessly seeking but cannot find.
Forever walking but getting nowhere,
trying to catch up but falling behind.

I'm trapped inside a lonely world,
longing for my freedom.
I stand amongst the distant crowds,
screaming, no reaction.
Nobody can reach me here,
I'm abandoned in the hurt
from my past.

Frequently touching but cannot feel,
desperately looking but cannot see.
Always listening but cannot hear,
cut off from the world around me.

Donna Lumsden (14)
Northfields Upper School

WHO IS ME?

Black, red, white, yellow,
Who am I? What am I? Where am I?
Yellow, blue, scarlet, red
Why am I? How can I? Will I let me?

Red, blue, scarlet, white
Am I even me?
Scarlet, white, blue
Who is me?

White, blue, pink
Can I let me have me?
Will I let me know me?
Blue, white, green
I wonder if I can talk . . .
                              weep?

White, green, peach,
What colour am I?
Can you see me?

White, green, indigo,
Can I feel? May I laugh?
Green, indigo, orange,
Can I taste the taste of love?

Indigo, orange, black
I, me, myself.
Be yourself!

Fiona Broni (13)
Northfields Upper School

IN THE 1900S

The Great War

In 1914 the war broke out,
And everyone began to shout,
Rats, lice, trench foot and flies,
As well as the filthy lies.
Thousands were killed at the Battle of the Somme,
Husbands and fathers they were all gone.

The Second World War

Not long afterwards another war broke out,
And once again they began to shout,
Hitler tried to gas all the Jews,
But later found out what it felt like to lose.

The Hippies

Then in the 1960s,
Along came the hippies
All flower power and flares,
They used to do silly things,
Like doing stupid dares.

The Man on the Moon

Then Neil Armstrong made his leap to fame,
And one big step for mankind,
And rocketed to the moon to see what he could find.

The millennium

Who knows what it will bring?

Becky Roberts (13)
Northfields Upper School

JOYRIDE

He had to run to clear his mind,
To leave all his troubles behind.
He ran to a clearing in a wood,
He sat down in that clearing, tired from the chase
He had won, he'd beat his troubles.
Now he could just think.

The clouds drew in around him,
Mumbling their threats, their promises of rain.
The weather began to mirror his mood,
The feelings he had, the pain.
He looked back to that fateful day,
The one he lost his friend
And he knew in his heart of hearts,
His pain was far from an end.

It started out as a bit of fun
Just a little trial run.
To see if it would give them a thrill,
Now looking back it gives him a chill.
They found it in a back street
A really pitiful looking heap.
They broke the window, there was no alarm
They tried to hot-wire it, worked like a charm.

They drove it to a deserted street
Then he chickened out, he got cold feet.
'What a chicken,' his friend cried
Just two minutes before he died.
The roar of an engine, the screech of a tyre
Then the street lit up in bright coloured fire.

The picture of that smouldering car
Still burned his thoughts and dreams
And he wondered all the time
If he could have saved his friend.

Brenden Delaney (13)
Northfields Upper School

BRACE

Braces can be different colours,
Silver, blue and purple.
Mums, dads, sisters, brothers
Different shapes, squares and circles.

First I'm snapping, breaking, bending,
I feel the pain upon me.
The pain comes back, it's time for mending,
Pulling, tugging just wish I could see.

I hear strange noises surrounding my metal,
I'm frightened, scared I'm all alone.
I'm frail, small, fragile like a petal.
I'd rather be strong, strong like a bone.

First I'm snapping, breaking, bending,
I feel the pain upon me.
The pain comes back it's time for mending,
Pulling, tugging just wish I could see.

It's time for eating, food flying around me.
I'm hurting, bruising, stinging like hell.
It's time for drinking, I'm burning. It's tea!
I feel like I'm empty like a broken shell.

Lisa Taylor (13)
Northfields Upper School

REMINISCING

When I was young
I used to play all day
I never got tired
And I got my own way.

As I got older
I learned to walk
Then a few months on
I began to talk.

I started nursery
It wasn't that bad
But when it came to leave
I was rather sad.

Next was lower school
That was really good
I learned to ride my bike
I wish I still could.

As I grew up
I learned more about life
Got a good job
And became a wife.

Now I'm old
I like reminiscing about the past
Because I know if I do
Then it will last.

Emma Clapham (13)
Northfields Upper School

HEAVEN

There is a place up above,
Where it's happy and full of love
That's where I'm going when it's time for me.
Up in Heaven that's where I'll be.
I'll be an angel and sit on a cloud
And play my harp to a nice little crowd.
I can look down at the hectic life
Full of hassle, full of strife.
I'll wear my halo with such pride,
No blemish or defect will I have to hide,
For up in Heaven we're all the same.
No one's a title, no one's a name.
When I'm there I'll be free of worry or pain
And one thing's for sure we'll meet again.
In a place that knows no time.
A place up above, that's yours and mine.

John Owen (14)
Northfields Upper School

WHITE

White is the colour of a diamond.
White is the colour of a sick face,
The moon in the night sky
White is the colour of eggs,
The colour of new trainers.
White is the colour of school chalk,
White is the colour of snow.
White is the colour of a deadly shark.

Carl Budd (14)
Northfields Upper School

THE OLD LADY

Scratched and ill,
Old and sad,
She wanders the streets,
All alone.
No one wants to know,
No one wants to see,
The old lady with only her bags.

She used to laugh,
She used to play,
But when she was a child,
She ran away.
Now she lives all on her own,
No hopes, no dreams,
Not even a home.

A cardboard box is where she lives now,
In the harsh cold streets.
No one to speak to,
No one to know,
Only the rats that scurry
In the gutters below.

Now she wishes she'd only stayed at home,
Back in the days when she was barely just born.
She could be happy,
She wouldn't have to roam,
If she had only never left
What once she called home.

Amy Burke (13)
Northfields Upper School

TOMORROW

I'll get you tomorrow
'I'll kick your head right in,'
Said the boy looking angrily
At me from the garbage tin.

'I'll get you tomorrow,
I'll hurt you so bad,
I'm gonna get you every day,
And make your life so sad.

I'll get you on the bus tomorrow,
And push you out of the door,
But if you tell anyone,
I'll beat you up some more.'

It's always tomorrow
But never today
I guess he's a coward
In his own little way.

Stacy Hutton (13)
Northfields Upper School

GREEN

Green is the colour of trees,
Green is the colour of leaves.
Green is the sign of illness,
Green is there colour of weakness.
Green is the colour of an emerald,
That can sparkle ever-so bright.
Green can be the colour of anything,
Anything you like.

Michael Greenwood (13)
Northfields Upper School

THE KITCHEN

A kitchen is a busy place,
Where loads of things are done.
Making food, washing clothes,
Kitchens can be fun.

Different noises fill the kitchen,
Boiling water, knives chopping.
The kitchen is chaotic,
When Mum's done the shopping.

The kitchen can be a family room,
A nice place to see.
If I didn't have my kitchen,
I don't know where I'd be.

First thing in the morning
The kitchen's where we meet.
Mum's making breakfast
I go in and take a seat.

Sarah Steffens (13)
Northfields Upper School

BLUE

Blue is the colour of freezing ice,
The gorgeous sun-filled sky.
Blue is the tears of hurt we cry.
Blue is the wavy sparkling water,
Blue is cold shivering lips.
Blue is welcoming and says, 'Come in.'
Blue is a shark hunting for food.
Blue is a furry polar bear snug in its sleep.

Louise Rowles-Griffiths (13)
Northfields Upper School

AN ANT'S EYE VIEW

As the queen took her stadium in the huge dark cave,
Thousands looked around following her gaze.
Gasps were heard as they saw what must be done,
Up the monstrous walls, to the ground under the sun.

Five volunteers stepped out from the shadows nervously,
All shaking, except one, the brave, the fearless, the infamous Curly.
He was the bravest of the brave, the cream of the crop, the icing
                                        on the cake,
Even the thought of him made most bugs quake.

The five made their way to the infinite wall,
Curly, the leader standing tall.

Using all six legs, they started their climb,
Going up carefully, taking their time.
Two of them lost their balance and fell to their death,
To the screams and the crying underneath.

The climb went on, they were on the ground,
All around, buzzing of bees, rustling of leaves and an
                                        unrecognisable sound.
Through the tall green forest they began to run,
But to their surprise, there was an eclipse of the sun.

They began to realise that this was no eclipse,
This was something that could make them go squish.
Then a massive post came down at great speed,
All except Curly were killed, brought to their knees.

The ground should be left unexplored, he thought finishing this quest,
Curly was no longer the cream of the crop, the icing on the cake or
                                        the best of the best.

Lawrence Willis (13)
Northfields Upper School

PENCIL CASE

Old, scratched, smelly and bad
I sit alone in Samantha's bag.
She used to love me I was cool
She chose me when she was small
She filled me up with goods galore
But all I could do was call out for more.

I made some friends with rubbers and pens
Even the ruler couldn't be cooler.
As my friends became old
I'd lost my touch, so I was told
Maybe it was my sides, getting rough
Even the rubber said he had had enough.

As time went on and my friends got worn
I dreamt of a new era, to be born
I dreamt of new pens and pencils too
I really wished my dream would come true.

Then one night here they came
It brought the feeling back again
Rubbers and pens they're all here
It felt like it was a whole new year.

Just as my life was back on top
A new pencil case came into the shop
I felt myself being put away
Never again to see the light of day.

Matthew Bandar (13)
Northfields Upper School

THE LIFE OF A PENCIL

Old scratched worn and bad
I sit in my box feeling all sad.
I sit in there day and night
Waiting for someone to show me some light.

Finally someone pulls me out
Where I have to listen to him shout.
He scribbles hard on my head
And this is time when I go to bed.

The ruler gets snapped,
The rubber gets worn,
I'll probably be next,
To be battered and torn.

I have made a friend,
The pen in fact.
He shows me around and
Teaches me to act.

He's the best friend there is,
The pen is that.
He helps me out
When I'm in doubt.

Old scratched worn and bad
I sit in my box feeling all sad.
I sit in there day and night
Waiting for someone to show me some light.

Ricky Parker (13)
Northfields Upper School

ALONE

I'm alone in the deep, dark cell
Alone and no one else
I hear people's voices
But can't work it out
No one can see me
No one can hear me
I'm alone in the deep, dark cell
I shout for help
Bang for attention
But no, I'm stuck,
Stuck in this mouldy, dirty cell
No one cares, no one listens
I'm alone in the deep dark cell
There's no light for me to see,
No food for me to eat,
No warmth for me to have,
Nothing for me to even live.
I'm alone in the deep, dark cell
My clothes are thin
Dirty and worn
My hair is like a woken up lion
My skin is like a sleeping snake
My shoes are torn, tattered and smelly
I'm alone in the dark death cell
I feel frozen, cold like ice,
I feel tired, isolated and hurt
I think and think, think what to do
But nothing will appear as
I'm alone in the deep, dark cell

I'm frightened, worried, will I ever get out?
Why am I here, who put me here?
I just don't know.
I'm here forever left to die
I'm alone in the deep dark cell.

Katie Neal (14)
Northfields Upper School

RUBBER

I'm a brand new rubber,
Bright and clean.
I'm the envy of the other stationery.
I take my place in the pencil case
And bask in all my glory.

I'm a grubby eraser
Corners worn down
I fit in with the other stationery
'I love SQ, I love Sue'
Is scrawled all over my side.

I'm a smelly old rubber
In two pieces now,
I'm laughed at by the stationery
As I crumble you hear me grumble
Till I cannot be used anymore.

I'm no more an eraser
Bright and clean
No longer a piece of stationery
Like the old glue, my life is through
I'm off to Stationery Heaven.

Nicola Botcher (14)
Northfields Upper School

RUBBER

Stuck in the dark day by day
Just waiting to fade away.
Here he comes it's time to go
I'll see you soon, 'Bye, bye Flo.'

I'm nice and clean but not for long
I'll soon by dirty just like John.
Flo's the ruler and John's the pen
I'm the rubber named Dirty Den.

Us rubbers and pens, rulers too
All together we're feeling blue,
Nowhere to go,
Nothing to do
We'll just stay here me and the glue.

There's hardly anything left of me now
I'm as small as I can get.
That's because I've worn away
And now there's nothing left.

Larissa Sheehan (13)
Northfields Upper School

OLD AGE

When I'm old and grey
I hope my friends don't stay away
As I will cherish them every single day.

When I'm old and grey
I will sit by the fireside in my old rocking chair
Thinking of the good and bad times.

Declan Hanley (13)
Northfields Upper School

YELLOW

Yellow is the colour of the sun in the sky
that brings out daffodils and crocuses in springtime.

Yellow is the colour of the walls in our room
and when we are relaxing it makes us feel nice and warm.

Looking out of the window we can see the change
of the leaves on the trees into golden yellow.

Charlotte Haines (13)
Northfields Upper School

WHITE

White is cold as snow and is the taste of vanilla ice-cream.
White is tasty as mash potato and is the colour of a blinding light.
White is the colour of a shiny car and is the colour when you rub
things out.
White is the light in the morning and is hot boiling radiators.
White is elegant like an angel and is big towering walls.

Paul Murphy (13)
Northfields Upper School

YELLOW

When I see yellow I see cowards and
wild forest fires burning at large.
The colour of a sandy beach on a warm summer's day
and the way soft butter melts on freshly baked bread.
The look of the sickly yellow yolk from a freshly fried egg
and the colour of bunches of bananas on a supermarket shelf.

Greg Winter (13)
Northfields Upper School

BLACK

Black is the colour of the beautiful witch's cloak,
it is the colour of a dark scary night.
Black is the colour of the blazer I wear
it is also the colour of my parents' hair.
Black is the colour of a room without light
but black is not a colour which shines very bright.
Black is the colour of a witch's cat
and is the colour of the vampire bat.
Black is the colour of very bad lies.

Matthew Moleski (14)
Northfields Upper School

BLACK

Black is the colour of shadows
lurking around at night.
Black is the colour of death and the
colour of long stringy liquorice.
Black is the mysterious colour
darkness and emptiness.
Black is the colour of a new pair of
shoes or the colour of danger floating
around the corner.

Chris Boyle (13)
Northfields Upper School

GREEN

Green is the envy of the jealous person's eyes.
Green is the seaweed on the incoming tide
And the look after really frightening rides.
Green are the leaves rustling in the breeze,
Even the spots on the moulding cheese.
Green is the emerald glimmering in its box,
Or the moss on the unmoved rocks.
Green is the clover we wish on for good luck,
And the colour of the American buck.

Danny Bright (13)
Northfields Upper School

THE WONDERS OF BONFIRE NIGHT

Guy Fawkes glowing on a flickering bonfire,
Fingers of flames, reaching higher and higher.

Fireworks soaring aloft in the dark, night sky,
Exploding their riches before their descent to die.

The children screaming with intense delight,
Expressing their amazement at this wondrous night.

Whizzes and bangs mingle with shrieks of joy,
Incoherent noises made by every girl and boy.

Sparklers spitting diamanté showers all around,
Sending puffs of smoke as they fall gracefully to the ground.

The dying flames bring the once raging bonfire to an end,
The smouldering guy's clothes are rags, and with the ashes they blend.

Adam Croft (13)
Queensbury School

THE AUTUMN

Leaves fell from the long dangling branches
and glided gracefully down
Whilst children all around the trunk,
wrapped in hats, scarves, gloves and all,
With rosy red noses and bright shiny cheeks,
Jumped and ran and laughed.

With a great huge pile of red rustling leaves,
They screamed and played, and threw the whispering leaves around
the trunk.

As they floated lady-like down,
Whilst the never-ending sky,
was turning purple to pink to a very dark blue,
Summer had inhaled its very last breath,
and winter was drawing nigh.

The morning brought the fog and mist,
 that blanketed the sleeping town,
With the early birds who flew now south,
the squirrels who hide their nuts and fruit,,
All readied themselves for the cold hard winter ahead
Which the amazing amber autumn brings, with wind, rain,
sleet and snow,
To ensure that the season shall clean the town,
With its bright white glistening gown.

So now the children stay warm inside awaiting the magical glow,
With chocolate cookies and steaming hot cocoa,
Thinking about what tomorrow will bring, what treasures they
will uncover,
They will find out tomorrow, now that autumn is here.

Leander Moore (13)
Queensbury School

FRIDAY 5TH NOVEMBER

What a terrible awful autumn
It had been so terribly wet.
I really could do with a special night,
Or any happiness ever could be under threat.

My arrival at this colossal park,
The calmness of the sky at night.
Bustling my way to the very front,
Nothing extravagent could hinder my sight.

Rockets banging, Catherine wheels sizzling,
This well and truly lit up the dull sky.
Spectacular described these amazing scenes,
Until sparks streamed into Dad's eye.

My night suddenly turned dramatically sour,
I was scared bad things could happen to me.
When fireworks finally ended with a bang,
I was relieved I could still see.

As the fire burned, it looked spectacular,
The smell of smoke forced a smile at last!
The rain poured down, the fire was out,
This night was declining, thick and fast.

Sprinting home like an Olympic runner,
I pondered as I had some tea,
Different thoughts raced into my mind,
I finally realised what should happen to me.

I crawled out of the window and scampered up the walls,
Regrets never even entered my head.
I struggled onto the roof and looked at where I'd jump,
Then I did it, screaming, and lay on my drive, dead!

Geoffrey Baines (13)
Queensbury School

AUTUMN HAS OPENED SEASON'S DOOR

Autumn has opened season's door,
And rainbow leaves cover the floor,
Branches reach out to snatch the cold, crisp air,
As the children run without a care!

Now the cold has settled in,
And the dark nights begin,
As animals run and hide,
The squirrels guard their food with pride.

The autumn air is fresh and clear,
Although the winter's very near.
Soon the animals will hibernate,
And fall into a hypnotic state.

As the golden sun disappears,
The trees drop their leaves with tears,
For now begins the colourful season,
When nature puts its autumnal robes on.

Autumn has opened season's door,
And rainbow leaves cover the floor,
Branches reach out to snatch the cold, crisp air,
As the children run without a care!

Lisa Ayres (14)
Queensbury School

THE BONFIRE

The excited family waits with great anxiety.
That little match to that enormous fire.
The little match is struck,
He screams and jumps and works his way,
To the top of the great fire.

His friends join him,
They throw a great party,
Joined all the while by those baby flames,
Who grow up and dance with their brothers and sisters
While the old flames retire to Heaven.

Their souls wriggle and wind their way into the
                                    dark night sky,
Those smoky old devils crawl their way through
                                    that old oak tree,
Wriggling, revolving, wringing the branches
                                    of their life.

The family is pulled from the sadness of winter,
Warmth and happiness from the fire burn away winter.
The fire has a protective shield,
It keeps the unwelcome whistling, whipping,
                                    whining wind at bay.

For that great finale the party reaches up,
That last lifeless leaf falls alone into the seductive fire.
Therefore, for another year the great fire ends.

Paul Crane (13)
Queensbury School

SCHOOL IN AUTUMN

Bells clanging
Children pouring out
Breaking the carpet of leaves
They start to scream and shout.

Crackling, crunching
Snapping, scrunching
Leaves being cast into piles
By little children, wearing smiles.

Red, orange
Yellow, gold
Leaves fluttering from the trees
Whooshing, whooping in the breeze.

Chattering, cheering
Screaming, shouting
Little children, full of play
Cheerfully putting the leaves away.

Bells clanged
Children poured in
Gossiping stopped, all was quiet
Just another lesson, about to begin.

Natasha Moulds (13)
Queensbury School

HALLOWE'EN

Hallowe'en. All Hallows Eve. A hidden meaning of evil?
Surely not?
It's a time for parties, a time for joy
When children dress up and go 'trick or treating',
A time for laughing and a time for smiling.
Evil?
But what if . . .?
What if it really *is* a night where the supernatural world
Meets our own?
A night where the restless dead return to haunt
And try to free their tortured souls?
When witches wave their magic wands -
Cast unearthly spells upon us?
When cold-blooded vampires
Rise from their terrible tombs
And walk amongst us
Once more?
Genies finally released from their prisons
By some fool rubbing a lamp?
Do sirens sing seductively to lure
Poor sailors to their doom?
Have werewolves waited for this night to
Howl and whimper in the moonlight?

Or is it just a night of fun?
A harmless joke for everyone?
In you my friend, I do confide,
It's up to you - you must decide.

Fabienne Morris (13)
Queensbury School

THE BATTLE

He stood there,
like an army general,
proud as a peacock,
strong as a bear,
no fear,
shrugging off foes as we do coats,
their hero,
the conker.

Crimson leaves cover the ground,
hiding fallen comrades.,
golden leaves litter the arena,
scent of victory fills the air,
all around are nervous spectators,
but he hangs there resolute,
then his adversary emerges from the gloom.

With the wind at his back
he attacks.
Full throttle, like a raging rhino,
speed increasing by the second,
head down bracing for impact, then . . .
Bang!

The overpowering energy is released.
Sparks fly! Shells crack! Careers ended!
In a second.
Then the wait, how is he? Does he survive?
Will good overcome evil . . .?
He stirs, he has *won!*
Sheer relief washes over his hard face
He has survived
Only to go through it again.

Russell Fairfield (14)
Queensbury School

PRINCE OF SORROW

The laughing, giggling, tittering has stopped
Our smiling summer sun has gone
No more games, no more clubbing
The party spirit has left.

Dreary and dull, sadness and gloom
Autumn's shadow engulfed us
Unhappy faces and burdened hearts
The prince of sorrow has come

Bare treetops with their bony fingers
Tripped and tapped on the window
While the whistling wind
Played joyously with the leaves

Rain fell miserably
Soaking everything in its path
While the angry thunder clouds
Threw down their electrical lightning bolts

Dreary and dull, sadness and gloom
Autumn's shadow engulfed us
But yet there is, still to come
The frosty figure of the winter king.

Kelly Yeung (14)
Queensbury School

AUTUMN IS HERE

Early morning mist creeps, swallows the scenery
in a blanket of crisp whiteness,
Harsh wind prowls restlessly, biting anyone who
challenges it deep into the bone,
Lightning rips across the sky greedily lashing
down at the ground,
Golden leaves shrivel and begin their gentle descent
to their waiting tomb,
Rain claws, savagely, at faces - cruel and sharp,
Ripe corn is cut leaving the ground naked and
embarrassed below.
Clouds shroud the sky leaving the world gloomy
and lifeless.
A subtle darkness enters the world,
A time of death and destruction,
Autumn is here.

Kirstie Morgan (13)
Queensbury School

GUY FAWKES NIGHT

In the dark of the night,
We wait in anticipation
As the first bangs and booms of the fireworks
Ripple across the rows of elated faces,
Choruses of ohs and ahs sound.

The fireworks whoosh into the sky,
Bursting like a shaken champagne bottle,
Its contents spreading rapidly across the velvet sky.
Catherine wheels and sparklers dance with glee
Lighting up the dark.

Rain falls,
The fireworks finish,
The bonfires burn out,
The evening closes in,
The end of an era.

Emily Farley (13)
Queensbury School

AUTUMN DAYS

I love the autumn best of all
when all the leaves begin to fall

Virginia creeper turning red
extra blankets on the bed

Walking through freshly cut grass
warming myself with hot soup in a flask

Frost on the window moving higher
another log upon the fire

Smoke swirls from chimney pipes
harvest fruits have all turned ripe

People walking dogs in the park
hurry, as the evening grows dark

A blanket of leaves cover the icy ground
crackling, crunching and swishing around

Days so short and shadows so tall
I love the autumn best of all.

Jenny Pooley (14)
Queensbury School

AS WINTER CREEPS NEARER . . .

Slowly summer's sweet scent is ebbing away,
The air is full of the smell of bonfires,
Glowing with warmth across the quiet countryside,
Icy fingers of trees, drooping down to the ground,
Losing their leaves like slippery, slithering
                              snakes shed their skin.

Fallen conkers among the crisp, crunchy autumn leaves,
Colours of red, russet and orange rustling upon
                              pearls in the wet, moist grass,
Squirrels busily collect nuts for the cold, long winter ahead,
Fruits of the world celebrate a golden harvest.

Children playing happily, smash their shiny conkers,
Birds migrate south for yet another summer,
Prickly hedgehogs prepare for hibernation,
As night falls, a thick fog blankets the high hills
Like a mother putting her child to sleep.
The sky is lit by sparkling stars,
And now like a snail, winter is bitterly creeping nearer . . .

Roshni Siyodia (13)
Queensbury School

AUTUMN

The lazy sun glows invitingly
Not bothered by menacing clouds

Leaves dance in the blustery winds
Children's laughs are heard as
                              conkers fight

Leaves become a colourful carpet
Trees prosper no more

Animals reign the blissful nights
Whilst crisp crunchy leaves crackle.

Laura Wells (13)
Queensbury School

THE JOYS OF A BONFIRE

Anticipation of the first big bang,
The first spark lit up the woodpile.
Flames licked the wood with vigour,
Grey smoke billowed into the open sky.

Warmth spread like a blanket,
Enclosing the people around it
In one cheerful wave.

Merry voices rang through the garden,
Like the sound of music.
The rich aroma of wet sticks,
As the roaring of the fire charred them to a cinder.

Sausages, sizzling succulently,
Steaming hot mugs of soup, warming chilly hands.
Potatoes baking slowly in the hot embers,
Teasing and tantalising the taste buds.

A noisy rocket explodes,
Showering tiny droplets of colour.
A Catherine wheel sparkling and fizzing,
Joyous expressions of people, standing and staring.

Caroline Tilley (13)
Queensbury School

FIRST FLAKES FALL

The warmth of summer seems to become ancient history,
Autumn mists loom ever closer,
Airy, green leaves turn to crispy, crunching oranges and golds,
Floating to the floor with amazing, tumbling grace.

First flakes fall,
They gently coat the outstretched arms of the tree,
Branches only possess a few orange leaves,
To cheer the blinding white.

It is now nearing winter,
Ground is hard and sharp
Plants and trees now lie bewildered, completely bare,
Animals remain sparse.

But soon the spirit of winter will reach,
A new season lies in wait,
To take over from the last,
As if it had never occurred.

Trees bright, fresh green leaves,
Will be revived by the warmth and rain,
Animals will taste the new spring air,
Before we start to plan for next Christmas.

Ruth Gray (13)
Queensbury School

SUMMER'S GONE, AUTUMN'S HERE, WINTER'S COMING

Scorching summer sun was over,
Autumn weather's arrived.
Frosty and misty mornings,
Moonlit night-time skies.

Trees and branches dying,
Becoming very bare.
Golden leaves have fallen,
Carpeting the russet floor.

Wildlife disappearing,
Ceasing to exist.
Animals are kept in hiding,
For a long, cold winter's rest.

Apples have rosy cheeks,
Like the children in the yard.
Children playing conkers,
In the cold and windy park.

Sitting by the spitting fire,
Eating baked potatoes.
Wrapped up in more clothing,
Woolly jumpers and warm scarves.

Weather's getting colder,
Snowflakes fill the air.
For the winter's coming closer,
And Christmas will soon be here.

Caroline Peak (13)
Queensbury School

AUTUMN IS HERE AGAIN

As the majestic sun rises,
A bird song so sweet echoes into the dawn sky.
I wake slowly and a familiar smell, allures me out into the garden,
Like stepping into a dream.
My surroundings are peaceful and serene,
I tiptoe quietly on the slippery morning dew,
A whisper trembles through me . . .
Autumn is here again.

Such awesome colours surround my toes,
A blinding glare of fiery orange and mellow yellow
dances around my eyes,
The last leaf falls from a leafless oak,
It gracefully descends like a snowflake falling from the heavens above.
I stare out into my garden and then further into the hills that lie beyond,
A sight so beautiful that it makes me feel sombre,
A tear of sadness lies on the brink of my eyelid,
Such a woeful feeling overcomes me and a single silver tear
tumbles down my cheek.
Ever so gently a breeze washes over me and with it comes its meaning,
Autumn is here again.

A season of pure mellowness,
Sleepy and beautiful is its nature,
It fulfils the dreams of the young ones who wish for a world
of happiness.
On freezing autumn nights come the fairies and demons of the night,
That fill infants' heads with tales of princesses and wizards.
For romantics it sings sensual, bittersweet promises of love
forever more.

To the restless parent, a time of self-discovery and finding answers
to question about life.
So as I ponder on the deepest thoughts inside me,
A little voice inside me whispers quietly in my ear,
Autumn is here again.

Samantha Taylor (13)
Queensbury School

AUTUMN

A full harvest moon is rising,
Though it is still only twilight.
The damp air ponders the way to go,
Leaving the clamminess of its touch.
Mist gathers around, comforting
And putting at ease everything in its path.
The warm and weary summer is but an illusion,
We are left with a steady and reassuring in-between season.

As night emerges from a devil's haunt,
The jocund atmosphere is turned to gloom.
The trees are like tigers preparing to kill,
Stalking their prey and eager to pounce.
The frightful, fearsome forest stands as a silhouette,
Along the skyline, with the faceless moon behind it.
Gusty winds cannot be heard above screeches and shrieks,
Which both subside at the break of a *new day.*

Alice Tunmore (13)
Queensbury School

THE TREES OF THE UNBIDDEN

The intermittent drip of the crumbly, crispy and crunchy
Assortment of diminishing russet leaves,
Tenderly float from the bony fingers
Of each officious and rime-covered torso,
Illustrates that autumn's nearing.

Spindly trees left scarred by cruel frosts.
Unrelenting winds wailing and chiming,
Reminiscent of convicts dragging their chains
Condemned to carrying their eternal burdens,
Exposed and unprotected from their sinful ways.

Early morning dew clings to networks of spider webs,
Linking each spindly branch to the net.
Precariously dangling on emaciated threads,
Shutting out the cold like Austrian blinds
On a dank, dismal and deserted night.

The shielded and desolate world of blanketing fog,
Emitting mysterious patterns and eerie shadows,
Incongruous shapes, dazzling and burnished
Like a majestic palace of shimmering white,
Before fading away into the distant mist like a mirage.

Nicola Golding (14)
Queensbury School

FUR COAT

Snared, trapped and strung up
waiting to die
A quick, swift movement of a blade

Skinned alive.

Sam Antoine (15)
Redborne Upper School

SOULMATES!

I like to think I'm a generous person,
although many won't agree.
I spend a lot of my time with one other person,
who is very good to me.

We share many similar opinions,
which is why our friendship is strong,
we also have similar ambitions,
but sometimes we feel these are wrong.

Our aims in life are simple,
as complication is what we hate
and ugly men don't appeal at all,
or being used as bait.

I hope we'll keep in contact,
as our lives go separate ways
and all our young ambitions,
will come true some happy day.

I think some time our paths will cross,
as we're obviously true soulmates
and this is my most important aim in life
to make sure that I find my soulmate.

Amy Walker
Redborne Upper School

DEATH

Is a tragic thing, cold and heartless,
Thoughtful and insolent.
Never forgiving, always hurtful,
Leaves your heart in tatters at the loss of your love.

Andy Purkiss (15)
Redborne Upper School

FIREWORKS

Light the blue touch paper; stand well back,
It'll go off soon with a whizz or a crack.
First it glows red and then it goes white,
I say to my mum 'What a wonderful sight!'
It roars like thunder and showers us with rain,
There's a mighty explosion then it starts up again.
Once more it goes skywards, erupting in showers,
Demonstrating the force of its hidden powers.
It screams like a siren and wails like a cat,
If it stops right now I'll eat my hat!
The sound grows louder, it'll all end in tears,
It reaches a crescendo so the whole neighbourhood hears.
The entertainment dies down; there's peace at last,
My baby brother's tantrum is now in the past!

William Nixon (14)
Redborne Upper School

THE CRUSH

Looking across the canteen I can see,
A boy who doesn't want to fancy me.
His hair is reflecting the bright sun rays,
And his eyes are hazel as they gaze.

He has now noticed us laughing at them,
But in a kind way, both me and my friends.
At two o'clock the bell rings four times,
This is when he leaves once again.

In registration my mind is so clear,
As he wanders through my head.
When he looked I felt a sense of fear,
Because to me he was so near.

When I think back at his face in the sun,
I know that he is my only one.

Gemma Brandom (15)
Redborne Upper School

EIGHTY YEARS ON . . .

E   ighty years ago today,
I   ndividuals fought in vain,
G   oing out and causing pain.
H   undreds of men were all dead,
T   heir friends had been shot in the head.
Y   et the war still went on,

Y   es, many of our brave soldiers are gone.
E   ven though it's over now,
A   ll the pain and memories go on.
R   etired today but still so brave,
S   omehow they managed to be saved.

O   verseas they had such hate,
N   ovember 11th 1998.

Natalie McCaffrey (14)
Redborne Upper School

A CHILD'S WORLD

Be silent my child,
No longer cry.
Wipe away the tears
And clear your eyes.

Stand up tall
And gaze ahead.
Look into the future,
The things behind you are all dead.

Think not to the past,
The horrors you have seen.
Once innocent eyes now reflecting
A carnage of death.

But the sky is now clearing,
The buds are opening.
Listen,
Can you hear the bird singing?
And although it is rusted,
The bell shall ring.

And you my child,
Shall blossom and sing.
Life's new beginning,
Nature's fresh new wonder.

The world is yours, my precious babe,
Make sure to enhance.
Learn from the past.
You are man's last chance.

Alix Courtney
Redborne Upper School

THE FORTUNE TELLER

She promised me a fortune,
She told me tales untold.
She told me of a prophecy
That slowly would unfold.
She enticed me with her wisdom
I believed she was a chum,
But all the good she told me
Was never to be done.
She spoke of only good things
Of all I loved to hear,
But she was telling lies you know
Of this much I am sure
For her ball was made of plastic
And this was crystal clear,
So nothing that she told me
Was true at all I fear.

Alex Hill (12)
Rushmoor School

MY POEM

Black and brown, red and green
these are some of the colours I've seen,

Up and down, left and right
these are the places I've been in flight,

Wedding bells and cheeping birds
are just some of the sounds that I've heard.

Kai Griffiths-Shilton (13)
Stratton Upper School & Community College

WALKING ALONE IN THE DARK

I   see cat's eyes glowing in the darkness
M y eyes begin to water as I stumble past a bonfire
A tree silhouetted against the night sky seems to
                                change shape as I watch
G rey shapes running around my feet
I   mages for in front of my eyes
N o one around, loneliness, silence
A nimals scuttling through the bushes
T he wind howls through the trees
I   magination, running wild
O wls hooting gently in my ear
N othing is the same in the dark.

Jennifer Stead (13)
Stratton Upper School & Community College

CONKER POEM

In late September
when I see everyone hunting
for conkers I think of all the
half-open conker shells
looking at me like lizards' eyes.
Then I pick one up.
Ripping the shell off the new born conker;
looks like a ball of chocolate - wet -
melting in my hands.
Smells like a brand new
mahogany table, straight
from the makers.

James Scott Davies (13)
Stratton Upper School & Community College

CHANGING SEASONS

The silence of winter is that of death.
Only an occasional rustling penetrates that awful silence.
Southerly winds bring the longed for smell of far off summer.
Cold wind chafes bare skin, as though it is just an annoyance.
Winds cry through the skeletal remains of trees, like that of a
                                                    wounded animal.
The bitter aftertaste of winter is like biting a chunk of lemon.

Sun glints off seagulls wings, sending brilliant flashes across the sky
Ocean waves lap against hard packed sand.
The ocean spray against bare skin is like the touch of a lover's kiss.
Far off sounds of laughter mingle with the gulls' cries and
                                                    lapping water.
The summer heat seeps into the skin, soothing you into a
                                                    peaceful slumber.

Alexis Cormano (13)
Stratton Upper School & Community College

AUTUMN

The red, orange, brown colours
make me think of a paint pot.
The towering trees dropping their fruit
like blobs of paint - conkers, acorns and seeds.
Small leaves, big leaves, round leaves,
long leaves and heart-shaped leaves.
But mind, there may be a little
round ball of spikes.
These things breathe life but you
would not know from the ball
in the leaves.

Keiran Williams (13)
Stratton Upper School & Community College

2000 AND BEYOND

I am now floating high
Way above the clouds
Into the world beyond
I can see clear in front of me
For many years to come.

For the world has changed
It's different now
We don't run or play
We fly and dance
We have no fights or wars
We only have friendliness and peace.

For the world has changed
For the people have changed
We think clearly now
We see what's happened
And what's going to happen
We know what we should do
Also what we should not do.
I cannot tell you how pleased I am
That we no longer have fights or wars
Or bullets and guns to shoot people with
It's a better place
A better life
For the world . . . has changed.

Jacqui Hart (13)
Stratton Upper School & Community College

NIGHT-TIME - AND WHY NOT TO SNEAK OUT OF BED!

It was night, time of fear, of fright
I could not sleep,
I tried many methods including counting sheep,
I jumped out of bed and to myself said,
'I shall go downstairs, for no one really cares what I do.'
So down I crept, as the household slept.

The window was open, the wind came in,
And through it came an awful din.
With it came a funny voice
So I listened, I had no choice.
'There's something there' it seemed to utter,
'What, where?' I began to stutter
'It's there upon the bottom stair'
I screamed, scared, yet I wasn't tainted,
Then without warning, I collapsed and fainted.

Clare Pulling (13)
Stratton Upper School & Community College

AUTUMN SURPRISE

They were so new and shiny
As if they'd been polished for days
I rushed around picking up every one I could.
The excitement was overwhelming
But then those curious balls of green spikes
Looking like tiny hedgehogs
I always wanted to pick one up
But never dared.
I wondered why they were there
And what they were?
What were they?

Nicola Massey (13)
Stratton Upper School & Community College

THE OCEAN

As the sun goes down and the moon comes up
The waves on the ocean go splish, splash, splosh
As the ships on the sea glide over the waves
The rock pools bubble with a shining glaze
The moon glows through the deep clear sea
Where sparkling fish swim happy and free.
There are rocks on the bottom of the sea-green ocean
Where the crabs and friends are still without motion
There is no light now, where the seaweed grows
Where the tiny, little flower plants pose
It is still in the ocean as everything sleeps
With sand on the shore, piled in big heaps
As dawn breaks again on another day
And the sky is clear with bright sunshine rays
As animals wake from where they lay
The day is busy with nothing at bay
And again as before,
The sun goes down and the moon comes up
The waves on the ocean go splish, splash, splosh.

Samantha Hope (13)
Stratton Upper School & Community College

FLEA

It's just not fair
I can't sit still on a chair
All I want to do is scratch
No one seems to care!

All I did was sit
And up you came and bit
At first it was fine
Now I'm in a scratching fit.

Oh little cat flea
Why'd you bite me
Three times on my ankle
Once on my knee?

Naomi Peters (13)
Stratton Upper School & Community College

HOW WILL IT END?

Our planet is dying and we just sit around,
Wasting valuable energy from the sky and the ground.
If only you'd think before you turn on that extra light,
And stop to ask yourself 'Does it really need to be on during the night?'
If the taps weren't left running all through the day,
There'd be much more water and a lot less to pay.
Before too long the ozone layer will be no more,
And onto the Earth the harmful rays will pour.
If only we'd stop using harmful CFCs
And unnecessarily cutting down those trees,
Because after all it won't be just us who'll die,
It will also be the innocent plants and animals - it's no lie.
So come on get your acts together,
And our race could live on this planet forever.
If you don't we'll either run out of our essential resources,
or the sun will come down hotter and simply scorch us.
In the end it is up to you,
It needs to be everyone - not just a few,
Who do their bit to preserve our planet,
If we all contribute, no one could regret,
Not saving our planet and ending up *dead!*

Daisy Whitbread (13)
Stratton Upper School & Community College

WINTER

Winter makes me think of Christmas
Dinner, presents, holidays and snow
Boxing Day is always a let down
But then it's to Wales we go.

Winters of blazing fires and hot chocolate,
Dark days and even darker nights.
Nan makes her toast on open fires,
Using candles to save the lights.

Winter still means school and buses,
Warm clothes, hot dinners, the lot.
Science takes on a new meaning,
Temperatures are cold not hot!

Winter's when we make our snowmen,
Sledges, snowballs, frost and ice.
Skating on the duck pond's dangerous,
But heading for 2000 - nice!

Gareth James (13)
Stratton Upper School & Community College

BEACHES

Beaches are sandy
Beaches are bright
Swimming in the sea
Fills everyone with delight.

Soft whipped ice-cream
Ice-cold drinks
Screaming, having fun
Who cares what anyone thinks?

But then the summer is over
The sun goes behind the cloud.
The nights get dark and cold
And the sea breeze gets ever so, ever so loud.

Donna Jakes (13)
Stratton Upper School & Community College

MEMORIES OF BONFIRE NIGHT

People stand like ice blocks,
As they rub their hands together,
Waiting for the fire to start.

When it starts burning,
People stand with their heads face up, to see
The fireworks bursting into bright colours.

Other people turn up to see,
The ashes floating into the sky,
Like fish floating to the water's surface.

People walk to the café stands after,
Smelling the beer and the soup, feeling
Like they were in a booth in a bar.

Other people edging nearer to the fire,
Rubbing their hands,
And hugging each other to keep warm.

Whilst I look into the flames,
Watching Guy Fawkes burn, then burst into flames,
The way he wanted others to die.

Mary Orchiston (13)
Stratton Upper School & Community College

THE SWIMMING POOL

When the temperature rises,
And I feel sweaty and hot,
The thought of cool water all around,
Is like finding an oasis in the sand,
So down to the pool I journey,
And armed with my swimming costume and towel,
I will slap on the suntan lotion,
And jumping in with one great leap,
I'll splash the people all around,
And cause a commotion,
Then I will glide through the clear water,
Hearing the laughs of children while they play,
Hitting the inflatable ball through the air,
And diving for it when it lands.
But after a few hours the water feels chilly,
And goosebumps prickle up on my skin,
It is time to get out and take a shower,
But knowing it will be there for another summer's day.

Lyndsey Garrill (14)
Stratton Upper School & Community College

FUNKY GRANDMA

Funky Grandma
Walking down the street,
Always says 'Yo'
If you happen to meet.

Funky Grandma
With her multicoloured hair,
Always ignores the
People who stare.

Funky Grandma
As healthy as a horse,
People say 'How?'
She works out, of course.

Funky Grandma,
Seems younger than me,
But in real life
She's eighty-three!

Alicia Harrison (13)
Stratton Upper School & Community College

THE PLAYER

I got up off the bench
and started to walk along the white tunnel.
It was a lot colder outside,
than in the warm dressing room.
I walked out onto the pitch,
to hear a roar, that sounded like thunder.
I could see my breath
and my hands were numb.
The ground was hard and damp,
as I made my way across slowly.
I took my place in the line,
which I had done many times before.
I could see at least eighty-thousand faces,
and those faces were watching me.
Then we were off . . .

Danielle Braybrooks (13)
Stratton Upper School & Community College

MY SNOW

In the midst of a cold winter
And Christmas holidays
Frost had laced the dirty ground
Like fresh bed linen.
Then, a long night's sleep and out of the window
The frost was now soft, like pillows and deeper,
Now it was snow, crisp and white.

I took a mittenful; the wet struck my hand,
And barely being able to judge, I threw like a frosted catapult.
As I turned my head, a blow struck,
Forcing my neck, like a fall on hard ground.
Then, up in the sky more white flakes were falling,
Each one different, like people of the world,
And opening my mouth, I felt each fall in,
Moist, yet almost warming in the cold of my mouth.

As dark clouds dominated the sky, it was time for bed,
Falling asleep, dreaming of new snow tomorrow
Awaking early, jumping out of bed,
I gazed through the window.
A disgusting taste and a sick feeling inside!
The roads and pavements now visible with only brown
                                        slush lazing in the drains.
Yesterday's snowmen doomed to melting,
Just the way I felt.
The cold was not comforting now,
Not without the snow.

Rachael Head (13)
Stratton Upper School & Community College

CONKER PICKING

Late September, with heavy winds these small round sacks
that hang on trees start to fall.
Myself and a friend go conker picking rarely, but we had
decided to pick until there was no more.

One day, in the middle of September, I was walking, when
it hit me . . . as I looked up, three fell in my hands.
Smooth, round, soft, like vulnerable babies were falling
from the sky into my clutches.
As I opened my hands to look at them, a bright light came
from the breaking open sea creature.
The more it opened the more I couldn't see the bright,
smooth, glossy conkers.

Thousands were falling all around me, some hitting me
by accident. As we started to gather more and more,
we kept seeing big glossy ones so we had to keep going.

We could see in the distance a bright glow with a trail of
small baby conkers leading to it.
As we approached the bright light winds blew leaves up
all around us.
Behind a bush was a gigantic conker as big as a school table.
As we leaned over to grab it we started to sink in
the wet quicksand full of greed. As we
went under never to see daylight again, we could
understand what was happening,
we were so greedy, taking all the baby conkers their mum
got her own back.

Rachel Louise Morris (13)
Stratton Upper School & Community College

CONKER PICKING

Early autumn, having light rain and sun
the conkers would appear.
As children from the near neighbourhood
would riot round their houses looking for
pots, pans, jars, anything which was cosy
to hold and good for carrying.
As they set out on their trek to the country
they pass bushes of which many conkers
have not ripened yet.
When they reached the woods, they would all split up
Searching for conkers, once one child got one
another would get two.
As you picked that first conker you start to notice the
glossy marbled skin and the rough jacket shell.
As the children began to walk home they realised
that they couldn't take their conkers home so the decided
to hide their conkers under the soil net to an evergreen tree.

A couple of days later, the children returned to their conkers
to find that their glossy, smooth, elegant conkers were now
covered in rot and smelt and looked like rotten fruit.

Leanne Hough (14)
Stratton Upper School & Community College

TRUE LOVE

Love is everlasting, like a velvet rose
And as does the grass, true love shall forever grow.
Just like an angel sent from above, we are
All blessed with the true ability to love.

Collette Marie Norman (13)
Stratton Upper School & Community College

CONKER PICKING

Late September when the ground is gold
with the leaves of the conker tree.
I looked up and saw the prize.
A spiky case glistening in the autumn sun
Suddenly a gust of wind whispered past my ear
which was red with coldness.
Then suddenly the shell dropped from the heavens
above. On impact the shell split like a
coconut on the damp grass.
Out of the shell came an almost evil eyes.
This eye was like a mahogany carving.
This conker was almost like a coin.
Shiny as can be.
I picked up my winnings and dropped
it into my bag.
When I net opened the bag there were
no longer any freshly polished conkers
but a green fungus.
The stench was the smell of greed.
My once glorious treasure was now plundered.

David Vaughan (13)
Stratton Upper School & Community College

MY ROOM

My room is my place where I like to be,
It makes me feel safe and comforts me.
When I am bad I get sent there,
Tidy or messy, I just don't care.
Everything's there where I left it before
When I want to be alone I close my bedroom door.

Phillip Bartlett (13)
Stratton Upper School & Community College

CONKERS

Collecting conkers is so much fun.
There're big ones, small ones,
brown ones, maybe even gold.
There was a round conker which was
so beautiful you had to have it, it was as
round as a ping-pong ball waiting to
bounce on the string.
You had already collected loads so you decide
to go home and have a conker fight.
You choose the biggest, hardest conker you found.
Popped a hole in the middle of the conker,
it's like when you take the cores out of apples.
Then string it up for battle.
As they hit each other cracking and splitting
until your brother's conker smashed into pieces
like glass being dropped on the floor, seeing it shatter.
The nice big conker had won and will win many more.

Holly Dennis (13)
Stratton Upper School & Community College

CAT

Creeping around the corner
As slow as can be
A cat looks around at its prey
Beneath the old oak tree.
Its eyes, like emeralds,
Its paws, soft as silk,
But all she is looking for is
A drink of milk!

Natalie Jayne Pearson (13)
Stratton Upper School & Community College

SUMMER AND WINTER

I like summer at the beach because it's
fresh and sweet.
The seagulls crying away and the sand
is soft on the bottom of your feet.
I can relax and sunbathe and get a tan,
I sit and wait for the ice-cream van.

I like winter, so cold and nice,
my nose has frozen
like a lake of ice.
People fight and roll in the snow,
not knowing that in a few hours
the snow will go.

Ben Lawrence (14)
Stratton Upper School & Community College

A HORSE ON THE SAND

The sun is merciless hooves
pounding against the sand.
No escape or fear it shows
Just a beat,
ongoing, strong.
Yet beyond the heat and
perilous sound of the beast
there is calm.
Winter, where all is frozen
like the night beyond the
chimney tops, where only
the moon is awake,
alive and watching.

Lisa Bly (14)
Stratton Upper School & Community College

WINTER DAYS AND SUMMER DAYS

W inter is an old man,
I n amongst the trees,
N o more little baby lambs,
T iny little bees,
E verything is cold and blue,
R eally old no longer new,

D eers and foxes
A ll come out at night,
Y early winter out of sight,
S pring is here again.

S ummer is hot in the midday sun,
U nder the old oak tree,
M y head feels real hot,
M ore often than not,
E nriched with the smell of the sea,
R ed hot and exhausted old me

D ays are long
A utumn's next
Y our time is up
S ummer's gone, autumn's here.

Tom Sizer (13)
Stratton Upper School & Community College

HAPPINESS

Positive thoughts, expanded mind,
Block out the wrong, put the worries behind.
Good and bad, always entwined,
Unravel the mess, see what you can find.

Don't look at the world and wonder why,
Eternal happiness, is it a lie?
Listen to advice and you'll get by,
Everyone's gifted, one day you will fly.

Vicki Coles (14)
Stratton Upper School & Community College

PUNISHMENT

Sitting here all alone staring at these four boring walls
I run my hands across the damp windows.
Looking outside I see the busy streets.
I'm feeling low, low as feelings get
Bored and upset, I try to get myself out of bed
But I ask myself
What's the point?
If I was a bird I would fly as far away from this dismal place as possible
Have I really been so bad?
For weeks I have wondered
Is it worth fighting for?
Day after day
Night after night
I sit here waiting, waiting . . .
I am tempted to escape
Tempted to run
Feeling lonely and empty I scream out the anger raging inside of me
Nothing to do, no one to talk to
And the silence of my room is killing me.

Jenny Willett (13)
Stratton Upper School & Community College

SUMMER

The sun is out, the weather is hot,
Summer's here and I like it a lot.

No school, no homework,
Swimming, having fun,
Time with my friends out in the sun.

Ice-cream, rides, chips galore,
Late nights and mornings,
Friends sleeping on the floor.

Summer's too short and as
The nights draw in
It's going to be time for school again.

Ben Bastin (13)
Stratton Upper School & Community College

LIFE

Life is a road that is never-ending,
Life is a bridge, separate for mending.
Life is a tree that will grow and then die,
Life starts as blank as the summer sky.
Life is all but a useful thing,
An old, dirty vase made of Ming.
Life is all greed and desire
The end of life, a burning fire.

Steven Harrison (13)
Stratton Upper School & Community College

A POEM FOR MY SISTER-IN-LAW

She stands there in a blizzard of spices
Floating back to Nigeria
To her life there,
To her family
To a very different world.

She is these spices full of flavour,
Sometimes welcoming
Sometimes angry
Sometimes even wistful,
But there is always something there.
A very special something.
Something warm, something beautiful
Something I wished I possessed.

Even her plane rises more than anyone else's,
She have a very special touch.

When her mind travels back to her
Little girl left still in Nigeria;
Her heart is warm.
Her heart is welcoming.
That special thing is always there.

Even when her skin and the colour
Of her wooden spoon mixes confidently;
She is graceful, she is beautiful.

When Teeya is screaming
She remains sweet and good (mostly)
That thing,
That special something
Is always there.

This very special thing is love . . . I give this to her with all my heart.

Julia Shields (15)
The Cottesloe School

HUNTER OF THE NIGHT

The antelope stands and stares into the thick of the night,
Black darkness surrounds the beast;
It senses danger looming close.

Roar!
Lions leap from the enclosing darkness,
Pounding across the dry plain,
Hunting down the antelope.

The antelope does not wait but springs away,
The lions, still persistent, chase it through the darkness;
Gaining ground every minute as the antelope tires.

On and on,
Until at last a lioness leaps through the air,
With a bang the beast falls as the lioness rips its leg away.

The chase has ended and the lions have their meal;
They sit crunching the bones and ripping the blood-stained
                                                carcass to pieces,
Until the antelope is no more.

Russell Pritchard (11)
The Cottesloe School

ART

The paper paid the paint
She was so very smart
The chalk chuckled with a cough
And they call that . . . art?

Sophie Burgess (11)
The Cottesloe School

A Life Of Imagination

The ground on which people walk
The sky, a sea of clouds entangled.
Air is a guide from centuries passed,
We breathe the air that kings, queens and dinosaurs breathed.
Rock festering into lava wiped out dinosaurs, as it may do us.
The twinkle of a raindrop, shared in fairy's eyes is spread all around.
The sound of a scream is enough to shatter a rainbow.
The laugh of a hyena could bring the world together, in peace.
The world is a locked door, who knows what's inside?
A baby's smile is worth all the money in the world.
The deep blue ocean is the colour of the night as it sleeps.
Your reflection, the difference between an odd and even world.
I hear the wind whisper its secrets in my ear, as it runs through my hair.
The faint sound of a life once lost still lingers in the air.
An imagination is your key to the world,
It holds secrets that will never be told.

Louise Davies (13)
The Cottesloe School